Praise for *Ageless Love*

Drs. Barbara and Michael Grossman have shown through their own experience that it is possible to fall in love forever and they have been **brave enough to share the quantum science that backs it up with a lifetime of evidence.** With my background as a therapist, I have seen relationships that seem to have everything going for them that still ended in divorce. If I had had this book and the science to share with each and every one of them then, *how many might still be together in a truly loving relationship?*

In *Ageless Love,* you will discover what the authors discovered–that there is something inherent in the heart/brain connection. **This heart-centered scientific approach to regaining trust, respect, and love brings a new type of relationship into these times of great change**. This book helps us look into each other's eyes as well as move in the same direction.

— *Patrick K. Porter, Ph.D.*
Founder/Inventor/Author
BrainTap Technologies

Ageless Love is really three powerful books in one. It not only gives you the knowledge and skills to have deep, long-lasting, intimate relationships but also how to create a life you truly love and **how to turn back the hands of time for your mind and body—all scientifically verified!** Thank you, Drs. Grossman for this life-changing treasure.

— *Debra Poneman*
Bestselling Author and Founder Yes to Success, Inc.

Ageless Love **opens you to the new world of science and spirituality** as seen through romantic relationship. It is a wonderful gift for couples and a wonderful resource for clergy who do marital counseling.

— *Kay Lindahl, CLP*
Author of *The Sacred Art of Listening*

Ageless Love takes its readers on a life-changing journey **guided by deep insights into romance, meditation, and enhanced by practical prescriptions.**

— *Stanley Krippner, Ph.D.*
Affiliated Distinguished Faculty
California Institute of Integral Studies
Co-Author of Personal Mythology

The *Ageless Love* book **weaves together an incredible journey of quantum mechanics, medical research, and fairytales** leading readers to a practical and passionate *Ageless Love*.

    I have been a clinical hypnotherapist for over 26 years. I love how they weave in quantum mechanics. I apply quantum mechanics to everything I do with my clients. Also, I was lucky enough to be at one of their live seminars. Dr. Michael and Dr. Barbara Grossman have beautiful hearts and their message is clear.

— *Kelly Fisher*
Certified Hypnotherapist

Ageless Love encourages us to re-examine our love relationships in deeper ways. Just as holistic health encompasses a healthy mind, body, and spirit, our love relationships are much more fulfilling when we optimize them in these ways. **You will be inspired to take your relationship to a new level of fulfillment and joy.**

— *Gretchen A. Reis, MD*
Integrity Wellness

The book *Ageless Love* **carries you on a journey to expand your mind and your heart** and inspires you to change your life and open to a bigger world of love.

— Benita Philips D.O.
Alive and Well Health

Drs. Michael and Barbara offer deep insights into the steps you need to re-create the intensity of romantic love in your life.

— Constance Crisp, M.D.
Anti-Aging Physician

Ageless Love **shares pearls of wisdom from Drs. Barbara's and Michael's 50 years of marriage,** 40 years in clinical practice, and 35 years of teaching marriage enrichment classes and meditation.

— Jennifer Landa, M.D.
Chief Medical Officer of BodyLogicMD
Author of The Sex Drive Solution for Women

Ageless Love **uplifts the reader's mind, body, and spirit** with practical prescriptions and deep insights.

— Bridget Krantz, ND
Doctor of Naturopathy

Ageless Love

The **Sexy** Science of **Falling in Love** Forever

PRESCRIPTIONS FOR MIND, BODY, AND SPIRIT

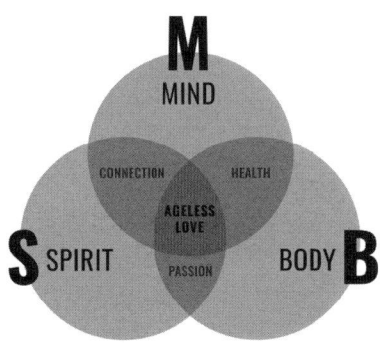

Barbara R. Grossman, Ph.D.
Michael J. Grossman, M.D.

Copyright © 2022 by Personal Development Enterprise, Inc.

Ageless **Love**

All rights reserved. No part of this publication may be reproduced, distributed, or transmitted in any form or by any means, including photocopying, recording, or other electronic or mechanical methods, without the prior written permission of the publisher, except in the case of brief quotations embodied in critical reviews and certain other noncommercial uses permitted by copyright law. For permission requests, write to the publisher, addressed "Attention: Permissions Coordinator," at support@agelesslovebook.com

Information provided in this book is for informational purposes only. This information is NOT intended as a substitute for the advice provided by your mental health or other healthcare professional. This includes any information contained in or on any product described in this book.

All matters regarding your mental, emotional, and physical health require professional supervision. Neither the authors nor the publisher shall be liable or responsible for any loss or damage allegedly arising from any information or suggestions in this book

Quantity sales special discounts are available on quantity purchases by corporations, associations, and others. For details, contact the publisher at the address above.

Orders by U.S. trade bookstores and wholesalers. Email support@agelesslovebook.com

The Authors can be reached directly at info@agelesslovebook.com

Manufactured and printed in the United States of America and distributed globally by agelesslovebook.com

978-0-9914353-1-9 Paperback
978-0-9914353-2-6 Hardback
978-0-9914353-3-3 eBook
978-0-9914353-4-0 Audio

Table of Contents

Preface i

Introduction to Ageless Love: Breakthroughs in Anti-aging Science ... iii

Section #1: The Mind: Understanding Romance — 1

Introduction 2

Chapter 1: The Breakthrough Longevity Factor 5

Chapter 2: The Mystery of Romantic Relationships 11

Chapter 3: The Real Story of Falling in Love: Fairy Tales for Adults ... 21

Chapter 4: Turning up the Romance: Partners Are Different 39

Chapter 5: Inevitable Quantum Jumps in Our Romantic Relationships: Stages of Adult Development ... 43

Chapter 6: The Mystery of the Divided Brain 55

Chapter 7: Living as a Wave 67

    Prescriptions for the Mind
    Living as a Wave in Your Romantic Relationship ... 69

    Rx #1: Understand life stages ... 69

    Rx #2: Make appointments for conversations ... 70

    Rx #3: Listening without interrupting ... 70

    Rx #4: "It would really make me happy if . . ." ... 70

    Rx #5: Understanding your differences ... 71

    Rx #6: Distributing chores and responsibilities ... 71

    Rx #7: Imagining your ideal relationship ... 71

    Rx #8: Learning skills for ageless love ... 72

Section #2: The Body: The Physiology of Ageless Love   73

Introduction   74

Chapter 8:   The Chain-Link of Physical Vitality and Longevity   79

Chapter 9:   Balancing Hormones as We Age   83

Chapter 10: Treating General Fatigue   89

Chapter 11: Testing and Treating Early Artery Clogging   91

Chapter 12: Treat Prediabetes and Prevent Aging   93

Chapter 13: Inflammation and Longevity   95

Chapter 14: Natural Treatments for Sexual Dysfunction   97

Chapter 15: Stem Cells and Exosomes   101

Chapter 16: Sleep Issues: Sleep Apnea   107

           Prescriptions for The Body
Moving Towards an "Ageless Body" and
Fixing the Weakest Link in the Chain of Health   109

           Rx #1: Check hormone levels   109

           Rx #2: Test and treat artery hardening   110

           Rx #3: Reduce inflammation   110

           Rx #4: Check for prediabetes   111

           Rx #5: Ideal blood pressure   111

           Rx #6: Reversing sexual disfunction   111

           Rx #7: Natural treatments for non-healing injuries   111

           Rx #8: Treating sleep apnea   112

           Rx #9: Motivation for anti-aging program   112

**Section #3: The Spirit: Connecting to the Field of
All Possibilities**   113

Introduction   114

Chapter 17: Spirit: Your Source for a Loving Future   117

Chapter 18: Meditation: A Technology to Experience
           Your True Inner Self   125

Chapter 19: Experiences in Meditation: Transforming Our Experience of Our "Self"	129
Chapter 20: Research on Meditation: Technology to Move into Our Wave-Like Nature	133
Chapter 21: The Foundation of Ageless Love: Consciously Letting Go of the Past and Living into the Future	137
Chapter 22: Epilogue	149
Prescriptions for the Spirit	151
Practices to Live in the Field of All Possibilities	
Rx #1: Learn deep, effortless meditation	151
Rx #2: Allow meditation bliss to direct your future	151
Rx #3: Giving up your complaints	151
Rx #4: Forgive everyone; write a love letter	152
Rx #5: Take our workshop: *Falling in Love Forever*	154
Appendix 1 - Studies on Bio-identical Hormone Benefits	157
Appendix 2 - Male Erectile Dysfunction	165
Appendix 3 - Female Sexual Dysfunction and Platelet-Rich Plasma	172
Appendix 4 - Stem Cells and Orthopedics	175
Appendix 5 - Meditation Research Articles	177
Appendix 6 - Science of Orbitals	184
Appendix 7 - Resources for Finding Doctors Practicing Anti-aging and Regenerative Medicine	189
Endnotes	191
Bibliography and Recommended Reading	194
Next Steps: Classes and Workshops	195
Other Books by the Doctors	196
About the Authors	197

Preface

by Dr. Michael Grossman

Barbara and I have written this book to inspire you and provide practical information and prescriptions for you to recreate your life and begin to live ageless love. Living ageless love means experiencing ongoing passionate love with a vibrant body filled with bliss and joy. We will show you how to create a new future that fulfills your deepest desires, how the new science of age reversal offers natural hormone replacement, stem cells and nutritional breakthroughs. We will guide you through the science of meditation as an age reversal technology. We will provide a map for how couples grow and change through the lifecycle and how to navigate these changes with new understanding and skills to develop your partnership in a way that matches and supports your individual growth.

Living ageless love means that you feel physical youthfulness and vitality throughout your physical life on this earthly plane. Further, it means you feel emotionally connected to love and joy with your partner, personal relationships in general, and connection to a higher, spiritual power.

You can read each section in any order you wish as each section, Mind, Body and Spirit, stands on its own. The Mind section will give you insights to see your romantic relationship in a new way. These insights will challenge how you think and understand romantic relationships. With these insights you can create intense, passionate love that will bring you to the experience of ageless love. The Body section provides a very practical description of actions to create a vital and youthful body at any age. We describe the latest scientific strategies to extend your life and maintain vitality.

The Spirit section will inspire you to open your heart and take steps to create an incredible future. We describe how the science and practice of meditation will support the process of bringing ageless love into your life now.

Enjoy,
Dr. Michael

Introduction to Ageless Love:
BREAKTHROUGHS IN ANTI-AGING SCIENCE

by Barbara R. Grossman, Ph.D.

This is a momentous time in history where science, medicine, and developmental psychology come together to redefine what is possible in a human lifespan. You won't read about this in the mainstream media or hear about this from our public leaders. As the old order is unraveling, the meaning of various scientific breakthroughs from physics and medicine to relationship research is filtering down and becoming digested and producing an enhanced way of living.

This book, *Ageless Love,* is about how you can grow your life and become part of this new age and promises to fulfill the inspired visions of all great cultures. We believe there are three new developments that are essential ingredients for practices that will allow each of us to participate in these new times. These breakthroughs correspond to developments that invite us to expand our mind, body, and spirit.

The first breakthrough comes from the new scientific understanding of the importance of the quality of your intimate personal relationships to your longevity. We want to teach you how to use your mind to develop your heart. We have taught crucial relationship skills to hundreds of couples that allow partners to regain respect and empathy for each other. This leads to learning how to negotiate life decisions about money, time, parenting, and in-laws, as well as how to help each other resolve childhood trauma. We all have these injuries and when we understand each other deeply and give and receive love in our personal relationships, our capacity for love is greatly enhanced for all life.

Ultimately, the heart supports the mind in developing ourselves in both these dimensions, and this harmony creates an integrated personality. The word integrated is related to the word integrity, and not by accident, because integrity is also crucial to our development as individuals and partners in relationship and community. Loyal and loving relationships also secure our children and support stable families.

The second breakthrough comes to us from longevity medicine. The last ten years has brought a new science of anti-aging to the public. It is not practiced in conventional medicine; it is not available through insurance. It's a new world of technologies that reverses the aging process through:

- *Natural hormone replacement*
- *The new field of epigenetics where genetic expression is changed through diet and nutrition.*
- *Stem cell procedures, exosomes and acoustic wave technologies that heal the body and often take the place of surgery.*
- *Very early testing for assessing health risks, and other technologies.*

These new tests and treatments provide an expanded vision for the human lifespan of healthy and creative activity. Health and vitality are necessary to our vision for ageless love.

By applying the breakthroughs from longevity medicine, you'll have the energy, along with the mental and physical vigor, to create a lifetime of love and creative activity. By applying breakthroughs to open your heart and by expanding your experience of yourself spiritually, you will be a blessing to your partner, your children, and extended family, as well as to your community.

For the third breakthrough, we want to direct your attention to meditation as a regular practice. We first heard about quantum physics in the 1970s when we learned to quiet the mind in meditation with a specific instruction that allowed us to transcend thoughts and connect with consciousness itself. Our meditation teacher coincidentally had a physics degree from a university in India. He was blending a traditional meditation practice with the language of science. Since then, the meaning and applications for quantum physics has expanded to provide a completely new understanding about how our universe is created from the quantum field, is permeated by that field, and how we creatively interact with that field all the time.

This means we each have access to creation and fulfilling our desires more easily than putting pressure on the material world, provided we are able to contact the quantum field. Most of the spokespeople who have been explicit about how to access this field through the mind have been teachers in the world of meditation. There are many traditions of prayer that have similarities to this process. However, they typically present their knowledge in the language of tradition and faith, not the language of science.

We have written this book to bring you the practical applications from these breakthroughs because we have participated in these developments over the past 50 years, and we have seen how each creative discovery weaves together with the other discoveries to create a new landscape for our lives. We want you to see the possibility of what we can create, individually and together, rather than pay attention to the chaos of the popular culture around us. We believe this is available to anyone who wants to develop themselves by growing their heart, their mind, and connecting their energies to building loving relationships. This represents a new wave of contributions we can offer to ourselves, the people we love, and our communities. With longevity, we can look forward to seeing the fruits of our efforts.

Best wishes for ageless love,
Dr. Barbara

SECTION #1

THE MIND:
Understanding Romance

by Barbara R. Grossman, Ph.D.

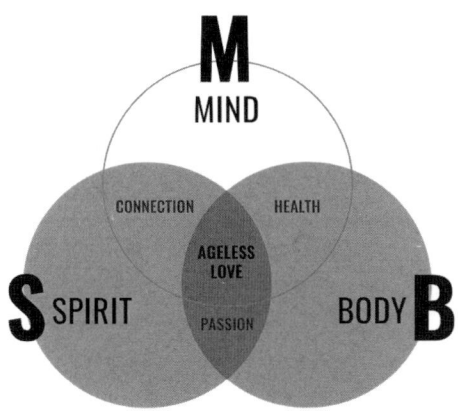

Introduction

How do two people who have loved each other and been willing to commit their hearts and lives to each other fall out of love within ten years of marriage? That was the question that dominated my mind about my marriage and my work as a psychotherapist for over 35 years. It is worth pondering because it is almost a universal experience in recent generations.

While the solution to growing a marriage through conflict and disconnection is deeply personal, I have come to understand it is virtually inevitable and impersonal in the sense that we each grow and change at differing time sequences, and we do not know how to talk to each other when there are unexpected differences.

When my husband and I got on the other side of our marriage crisis with the help of wise mentors, we taught relationship courses that trained couples in the essential connection and conversation skills to understand each other and nurture their differences. Our couples gained tangible benefits from our training. We also educated our couples about how adults grow at different paces over the lifecycle and how this affects our connection as partners.

Yes, development does not end at 18 or 21 years old; it continues over a lifetime. This accounts for the changes in perspective over time that have nothing to do with personality. We need to understand our evolving selves and our partner over time, as well as learn the art of listening and sharing. We are pleased with how we have supported our couples on their journey together.

In recent times, we have discovered a deeper understanding of how relationships decline. This bolsters what we have been teaching and comes at the dilemma from a different direction. Of all things, the revolution of quantum physics offers a reflection on the current state of our culture and the trapped and unsatisfying conversations we have with each other.

What I often tell a client after we've had a discussion about where they feel stuck with their partner is that they have two choices: they can be a particle or a wave. Their wave nature is their full embodied spirit with open heart, or they can contract themself and become their particle nature that is defensive, hurt, and perpetuates the problem. Someone has to volunteer to be a wave to change the dynamic.

I usually spend a few minutes describing how an electron can have the dynamic of an expansive nature as a wave or the contracted nature of a particle, and how it happens that an electron becomes a particle when it is observed by a scientist. My clients become inspired to maintain their wave nature in the face of whatever accusations and complaints their partner verbally throws at them. In this metaphor, the partner is the scientist measuring their spouse presumably to make an accounting. The accounting, of course, is a complaint or an emotional reaction that couples voice to each other. It actually is not a metaphor; it is what partners do when they are unhappy. With this coaching to maintain their wave nature and not succumb to measurement, my couples regularly report breakthroughs in their conversations at the next session. It is understood that this is a taste of possibility and the couple needs more training to make these kinds of conversations a reliable feature of their relationship.

The Mind section is where we share the relationship repair and growth that we believe couples universally need. These chapters also explain how the predicament we are in with our romantic relationship is not personal at all. It is inevitable given our culture and the dynamics of our individual development in recent generations. It is not personal in the sense that most couples will experience these earthquakes in their relationship, and the only way through this is by taking personal responsibility. It is a lot easier to move forward when you stop blaming your partner or yourself.

Your wave nature is your awareness of the fullness of your self that is connected to the Great Being of the universe. When you remember who you really are, it is easier to hear how you may have hurt your partner's feelings or fallen short in your promises. You can even hear their contracted state of crankiness and irritability which is the condition of a particle. We all get like that when we lose our experience of our full self. It only takes one of you to remember your wave nature and to offer love by listening and asking what your partner needs. This is the place where you can negotiate, and commit to new behaviors and reconnect.

My clients can deliver on their wave nature from our brief conceptual conversation about how they live moment to moment in one or the other of these two dimensions, and the choice to be a wave or particle is theirs to make. It helps to role play and I do that in session briefly. The *Falling In Love Forever* course we teach expands on this practice and adds additional skills. Learning meditation also develops the capacity to live as a wave. We address how this works in the Spirit section.

As always, we wish you great love. Your love for each other and your harmony together affects your own health and well-being along with your children's, your parents', and your community. You commit to the journey when you join your lives together. We want to show you how to deliver on your promise. This book approaches the vision of ageless love through the mind, body, and spirit. Your journey integrates all of these dimensions.

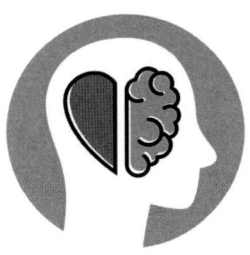

CHAPTER 1

The Breakthrough Longevity Factor

We begin with the mind. Physics and its exploration into quantum mechanics have given us a new understanding about the mind, meditation and the parallels of quantum theory and consciousness in our practical daily life. Our brain is an extraordinary manufacturing plant of signaling factors and hormones that spread throughout our body. Although there seem to be so many components to happiness and well-being, it really boils down to the mind and heart. They are fundamental to the health of the body and to pioneering work with longevity. What we share may surprise you.

What would you say is the most significant factor in healthy aging? Genetics? Wealth? IQ? Cholesterol? Obesity? The quality of personal relationships after the age of 50 was the most important factor in longevity according to an 80-year Harvard study of over 800 men.

Since 1938, the Harvard study pioneered by George Valiant, M.D. and known as The Grant Study, has conducted continuous research on a diverse group of men and their descendants to answer that question. Half were sophomores at Harvard College and half were from the poorest sections of Boston. The study involved lengthy interviews every two years with each participant and their family members, along with an evaluation of their medical records. This study is unique because it was conducted continuously over 80 years. Most of the participants have passed away, but the data is dramatic in evaluating length and quality of life. Regardless of genetics, social class, race, IQ, or medical risk factors, the study concludes that satisfaction in relationships is the most important factor in staying healthy and aging well.

Dr. Robert Waldinger, psychiatrist and professor at Harvard Medical School, and Director of the Harvard study from 2005, goes even further to say that good relationships have a protective effect on our brains. "Good relationships don't just protect our bodies; they protect our brains from deteriorating," said Waldinger, in his 2015 TED talk, "And those good relationships, they don't have to be smooth all the time."

Thus, the pathway to longevity is through healthy relationships, and the pathway to healthy relationships is a mind that is open to the change and flow of relationships over time, and a body that provides the energy and vitality for this development. Further, we are learning the parallels in physics about the dynamics in relationships that, to quote Waldinger, aren't "necessarily smooth all the time." Wave and particle theory, which we will soon discuss, reflects the kind of dynamism found in genuine, lasting relationships.

Creating longevity, then, requires intimate relationships where we can develop both the mind and the heart. The most intimate relationship is the romantic marriage relationship. There are many challenges in our postmodern life to create fulfilling, romantic partnerships. The roles for women have changed since the introduction of the birth control pill. Both men and women are working. There are less clearly defined roles for men and women. Divorce has been made easy. The level of busyness is increasing. Technology has diminished our face-to-face contact. How to maintain a fulfilling romantic partnership requires a deeper appreciation of the skills necessary.

The latest revelations in physics about the fundamental nature of our universe are metaphors for what we see in the challenges of romantic relationships. There is a need for movement, flexibility, mystery, and adventure represented by the wave nature of subatomic particles. But there is also a need for fixed modes of operation, of stability and security as represented by stable orbitals of electron pairs. How can we use these discoveries to shed light on the very real and challenging dynamics of relationships in order to propel our longevity?

In past generations, marriage was an automatic institution that could endure without emotional passion. It offered a stable and secure orbit for human pairs. But now we expect much more in marriage. We expect respect, partnership, along with intimacy and passion to continue over time. We now have deeper expectations for the experiences of the heart. We long for the wave nature of the subatomic particles that ensures the success of pairing. Without it, we can lose our way. When we lose that intimacy and passion with our partner, it is easy to look for it elsewhere. Divorce is accepted in our society. Multiple marriages are common in a lifetime. Role models of intimate, ongoing romantic passionate marriages are few.

Developmental psychology adds another perspective about the natural changes that occur over a lifetime as we grow in maturity. Understanding how adults develop emotionally and cognitively will provide a deeper appreciation of what it means to fall in love and stay in love forever. It does not always mean a happy, stable relationship. Rather it means a dynamic and evolving relationship where the mind and heart are each stretched and expanded over time. This requires a deeper vision for marriage and greater skills for maintaining intimacy. Since 1986 we have been developing classes and teaching hundreds of couples the skills that allow romantic relationships to become more intimate and heal each partner's childhood wounds. This allows the couple to restore and enrich the feeling of love and passion they had when they first were courting.

It is thrilling to see how science and the world of physics, which seems so far from the world of relationships, actually reflect the emotional dynamics we have been teaching for years. Not only does understanding wave and particle theory serve as useful analogies, the discoveries in those fields may also help deepen our understanding of how to be more successful in romantic relationships. More about quantum theory and relationships will come later. For now, it may help to know that in wave-particle physics, energy from subatomic particles like electrons and photons can behave as a particle or a wave.

When a scientist puts his attention on a subatomic particle to measure it with a mechanical device, the subatomic particle will collapse its wave function. The wave becomes a localized, knowable, and measurable particle. However, when it's not being measured, it remains unlocalized and in motion as a general possibility. This is an essential part of the mystery of the wave-particle dilemma of quantum science. Conscious observation for measurement changes the nature of the subatomic entities.

In a similar way, an individual can be fixed like a particle or flowing like a wave, depending on the emotions, circumstances, and awareness at the time. When we are stressed by responsibilities or accused of being less than our ideal self, we are likely to collapse our wave nature and behave like a particle. A particle is contracted and material. The metaphor in human terms suggests it is defensive and self-limited. There is no space for heart and movement. The wave in human terms is fluid and expansive; it can listen and respond with heartfelt generosity. We will develop this parallel so that you can see the meaning of the challenges in your relationship and the opportunities that your relationships provide for your development. So how does the wave and particle nature of subatomic particles apply to romantic love?

What first attracted you to your partner was your affinity as personalities, as well as an unconscious intuition that this partner could potentially heal your unresolved hurts, fears, and emotional blockages by providing you with what was missing from your childhood. There were similarities and there were differences in your personalities and life experiences. This provides the dynamics of the relationship and the pathway to your future development.

Falling in love is a life-changing experience where partners begin by meeting each other dynamically as waves. There is so much we don't know about each other that we exist for each other as possibility. The project of staying in love passionately as we become more known is a journey. In this section on the mind, we will take you on that journey to see the vision of how you can engage in the process of knowing each other more deeply while you develop as an individual, and at the same time, maintain and grow your connection as a couple. In the chapter on prescriptions for the mind, we will describe the skills needed for creating an ongoing, passionate, romantic partnership. This entails learning how to maintain your wave nature as your relationship involves more practical responsibilities.

We want to inspire you to use your intimate, romantic relationship to grow your heart and mind and bring fulfillment to your life. Being happy is a side effect of living a fulfilling life. A fulfilling romantic partnership continually presses you to grow and develop. Growing and developing is an ongoing challenge that doesn't always feel comfortable. However, your effort will pay off with unmatched joy, stability for your family, and extended life expectancy.

The Uniqueness of Romantic Relationship

Romantic relationship is a fiery relationship. Relationships of parent-child, brother and sister are like a deep ocean where the connection is always there. If you don't see your parent, child, sister or brother for a long time, when you see them, you are right back to where you were: listening and sharing and enjoying who they are.

Romantic relationships are different. If you don't see your partner for a long time, it takes time to rekindle the intimacy that you once had. Romantic relationships need constant heat, attention, touching, and sharing or they lose energy. They are highly dynamic and dramatic in the same way that quantum energy is constantly moving, reforming, changing and non-localized. If you or your partner are too fixed—more particle-like—unwilling to keep growing, then your romantic partnership will gradually lose its passion.

Romantic relationships will change over a lifetime. They will not stay the same. If they are staying the same, they may get stagnant; you may grow apart and you may find that others begin to kindle that romantic feeling. In quantum mechanics we know two electrons can travel in the same orbit only if they maintain equal energies and opposite spins. The purpose of this book is to explore ways to find balance—you and your partner's unique balance at any moment in time—through strategies and a deeper understanding of how love, longevity, and the role of consciousness intertwine.

QUESTION TO PONDER:

- *Do you feel the continuing passion in your romantic relationship or has some energy faded?*

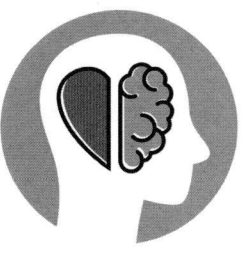

CHAPTER 2

The Mystery of Romantic Relationships

The renowned relationship researcher, John Gottman, reports that if there are more than 11 to 1 positive to negative interactions between a romantic couple, romantic passion begins to fade. On the other hand, if there are less than five positives for each negative interaction per couple, romantic passion also begins to fade.[1] How can this be?

The answer is: romance is a delicate balance between stability and mystery, and between security and adventure. Too much agreement and similarity within the relationship is boring. There is no stretch or ongoing learning. There are no edges that require deeper listening to understand. This translates to no growth and no distinctions of individuality. On the other hand, if there are too many differences, not enough affinities, this will also diminish the romantic connection.

Quantum mechanics offers a metaphor for this dynamic. When an electron wave becomes a particle, it becomes localized and easily known. The scientist observer knows the particle's direction and location. It is now predictable. There is no mystery or excitement. On the other hand, when an electron is in its wave nature, it is unknown. Its future position and direction are unpredictable. The wave form of energy maintains mystery.

Maintaining mystery in your human experience means allowing your wave form of energy to blossom where you are continuously growing and unfolding your personality. In our wave nature, we are the best version of ourselves, and it is in our wave nature that we generously appreciate our partner, and experience connection. It is the secret sauce of a romantic relationship to activate your wave nature. Here you are committed and defined as partners, like paired electrons, yet you are not entirely known or predictable.

The breakthrough in the science of quantum mechanics was discovering that a wave becomes a particle when researchers observe and measure a subatomic particle like an electron or photon. As I have said earlier, in a relationship, if we allow the critical observations of our partner or any emotional upsets to localize us, we too become a particle and lose the dynamism of our wave nature. We also become a particle when we allow past memories of upsets to recreate feelings in the present. We contract ourselves and become an object and we are predictable. This has many consequences for our development and the evolution of our relationships. In practical terms, as a particle we become defensive, we lose the awareness of the wholeness of our personality and life experience, and our generosity for listening and responding disappears.

If we understand the possibilities of our wave nature, we can understand the movement of points of view over time. This helps us understand ourselves and listen to our significant others with less fear about disagreement and differences. As human beings, we are in movement. Our position in any given moment is unknown, though not irrational. In physics, the scientist can graph the possibilities of the wave's orbit, but the scientist cannot know for sure the direction or location of the wave.

The wave can expand or contract its orbit; its movement is responsive to its environment. The particle is more fixed, more known. It is the difference between responding and reacting in a conversation. The wave, in this analogy, is more authentic and unpredictable; the particle is more reactive and the wholeness of its personality is contracted.

This is great news for those who have satisfying marriages and an incentive for those who don't. But what does it take to create a "good" marriage? What if you no longer feel in love with your partner? What if you are angry, withdrawn, or distant? Or, you feel more like roommates and you are planning your escape? What is really important is knowing how to use this knowledge to build, strengthen and transcend these patterns, habits and pitfalls. At the end of the mind section, we have specific prescriptions that will provide skills to recreate the passion of being in love. In addition, we have a list of resources that will guide you in gaining the skills.

The Physiology of Longevity: Reducing Chronic Stress

While the research on how important the quality of relationships is to our longevity is revolutionary in the field of medicine, it should not be surprising to those who understand the effects of mood and emotions on the physical health of an individual. Let us now describe why relationships affect longevity.

Every thought contains some emotional content which then creates some chemical change in the body. Many thoughts have a lot of emotional content, and those thoughts can have a considerable impact on the physiology.

For instance, if we see any perceived life-threatening danger, this will automatically set off an intense reaction called the fight or flight reaction. We immediately experience a surge of adrenaline that increases our heart rate and blood flow to our muscles. The blood flow to the internal organs and higher brain functioning turns off to allow us to focus on the here and now, to find the equivalent of the nearest tree where we can climb to hide. A corresponding reaction turns off all systems not needed for immediate survival. This includes our digestive system, our immune system, our repair and rejuvenation system, and most parts of our higher thinking in the brain. These functions are not needed for survival.

In the quantum physics analogy, the electron is in the field of all possibilities when it is a wave. It can move in any direction and appear in any location. It is quite undefinable. When the electron is pushed to become a particle through the impact of focused, measuring attention interacting with it, it becomes localized in a certain position with a certain direction. This is what happens in our own lives when we interact with something that upsets us emotionally. We become localized like a particle when we feel unfairly measured by our partner or we measure ourselves with self-criticism. Our responses become predictable and contracted in both our thinking and feeling. We block our own potential, our partner's potential, and the potential of the relationship. Creative solutions become unavailable. This blocks the experience of love. It also, as we will discuss later, affects our health.

The problem with the stress response and feeling like a particle in our relationships, is the stress is likely to be chronic as our relationships are ongoing. There are very few lions and tigers threatening our survival these days. However, there are frequent negative moods, ongoing emotions, and thoughts in our romantic relationship that produce stress. Reducing stress is critical to our health and longevity. A large percentage of medical visits are directly related to stress accumulating in our bodies. It is therefore not terribly surprising that good relationships, particularly that important romantic marriage relationship, is critical to health and longevity.

The good news is that we can change the direction of our health and longevity by working with our partner and learning to turn on the physiology of love. The physiology of love allows us to feel like a wave as it reduces stress hormones and increases the hormones that relate to longevity. Besides reducing cortisol and epinephrine which are stress hormones, we increase the hormones of love: oxytocin, dopamine, and vasopressin. These are hormones that relate to the experience of an unbounded wave feeling of love, feeling close, cuddly, and happy.

Feeling in love, the feeling of our wave nature, is much more than just a reduction of stress hormones. We actually turn on genes that create longevity and turn off other genes, some of which create illness. The genetic programming that we received from our parents is only one possible software application of our genetic inheritance. Our genes can be altered or changed depending upon our thoughts, emotions, and our lifestyle. We will describe this in more detail in Section #2: The Body. Ongoing moods can stabilize as temperaments that later become permanent personality traits. We can change these too, and we will show you how to do that in the following chapters.

Love feels good, not just because we are happy but because we experience our wave nature with all possibilities of joy and happiness available. Being in love changes our physiology and invigorates our health and vitality. When you feel that all possibilities exist in your world and you can live into your future which is unknown, mysterious, and delightful, you are taken out of the world of fear and limitation into a new world of adventure and love.

There is good news for those who are not experiencing this wave nature of happiness in their relationship. It is possible to reignite love and passion even if it's been gone for a long time. You can still create satisfaction in your marriage and become the loving, caring, intimate partner who will satisfy your partner's needs and get your needs fulfilled. We know. We've been there. And we will share later what dramatically changed the dynamics of our marriage.

The concept requires that we appreciate a loving relationship as much more than just being happy. It opens you to the joy of an unknown future rather than being burdened or constricted by the known past. In the beginning of a relationship, we are likely to be spontaneous and less restricted in our personality. We are a mystery to each other. There is a delightful quality of openness that allows the relationship to unfold. The unknown future of the relationship beckons us and we are excited to step into it. The unknown is an opportunity for adventure and growth.

There are couples who fall into predictable patterns of behaviors and conversations where they are not sharing their deepest thoughts and feelings. Partners in these relationships are vulnerable to being distracted by individuals outside of the relationship who offer new experiences of engagement. This is a common problem that shows up in a therapist's office. An outside romantic interest is not necessarily the death knell of a committed relationship. Usually it is not.

Just last week a client admitted his misstep into the world of cheating. He is a good man, and disappointed in himself. He proclaimed, "It is not about me not loving my wife. I love her deeply. It just got so hard to be open and spontaneous in our conversations. The other woman responded to me and I felt alive with her energy, and I responded back." Disloyalty in love creates chaos on top of whatever else isn't working in the relationship. It is the hard way to learn to be open-hearted with your partner, and to be honest and available for adventure. Let us look more in depth about what it means to fall in love romantically so we can understand what it takes to sustain ageless love.

When you first were getting to know each other, and you did not know what the future held for the relationship, you were likely more open to discovering the unknown about your partner. You were interested in learning about them. You experienced attraction and you wanted to know all about their history, their interests and values, and explore your similarities and differences. If your values were aligned on important preferences and the conversation had a depth of authenticity, chances are you felt connected and saw a potential for this relationship to provide both respect and love. There are other dynamics involved in growing attachment, to be sure, but this is the first hurdle for the prospective relationship.

Notice the importance of differences as well as similarities and how it represents each partner's desire to feel meaningful affinity, and to be accepted and loved as individuals. The dynamic of similarities and differences is another way of experiencing the predictability and mystery dynamic. Over time we change as individuals when we are in a relationship. One partner may try to please their partner and adapt and accommodate to maintain the relationship. Or, one of the partners may pull back emotionally and insist on having things their own way. Meanwhile, the couple has collapsed the dynamic of mystery, and now the need for predictability dominates. This leads to a loss of "feeling in love."

You may be wondering, why is this inevitable? The answer is: the skills that brought you into your most important relationship are not sufficient to grow the relationship over a lifetime. Creating ongoing ageless love requires both a big vision and many skills. Romantic love is not designed to be a smooth ride, but it is a path to the deepest fulfillment of life on this earthly plane.

We are like our partner in many ways and we are also different. One is outgoing and bubbly, and one is quiet and inward. One may be careful and cautious, and one may be adventurous. At the same time our energies harmonize into a state of oneness where we are no longer distinctly separate. Empathy is easy, and our connection is emotional, physical, and spiritual.

This parallels the two electrons who occupy the same orbital in the quantum field. An orbital holds one or two electrons. This is what the atom wants, and it draws the electrons to its orbital. There are never more than two. When there is a pair, they have equal energies, equal negative electric charges and always have opposite spins.

The nucleus of the atom with its positive charge dynamically attracts the negatively charged electron pair to the orbital space around the atom. The electrons are unified in their electrical charges, their equal energies, and their shared orbital, and differentiated by their opposite spins.

The dynamic of two electrons in orbit together in physics should not be understood as codependency. These are autonomous electrons who participate with each other in a deep energetic connection while they hold their own space and maintain opposite spins. As individuals, we experience a magical connection at the outset of a romantic relationship, but the probability is that in a finite amount of time, we move out of this unifying connection and become individuals again and experience disappointment, disharmony, or simply assert our independence.

This falling in love process in our human experience is automatic and, for the most part, outside of our conscious awareness. The challenge for partners is how to maintain this connection of affinity and differences throughout a lifetime.

Love is the Moving Force for Creative Activity in our World

Let's go deeper into this world of quantum physics, and later, the Newtonian world to see how relationships work. Atoms demonstrate a consistent desire to have electron pairs in their outer shells. They always have electron pairs in their inner shells. The total number of electrons always equals the total number of protons, except they can share electrons in their outer shells with other atoms. It is always only two electrons that share an orbit. This is a metaphor for how our universe is built on pairing couples, just like our human world.

Why do atoms desire electron pairs in their outer shell? Current science believes the electron pairs are more stable and have a lower energy formation for an atom. These electron pairs are what create the dynamism of all molecules in the universe and all the molecules of life. This remarkable pattern suggests there is an inclination for partnership in all living things. This is the nature of physical reality and it parallels the desire of humans to have romantic partner pairing.

The atoms, with their desire to have paired electrons in their outer orbits, move everything in our world to create the complex molecules of life. An atom that has any unpaired electron in its outer shell will seek a partner to share its single electron. (See Appendix for oxygen molecules, water molecules, and molecules of life made up of carbon chains.)

Quantum science is a relatively new discovery from the 1920s and its dynamic meaning has not been digested by our culture. Our cultural consciousness continues to be shaped by Sir Isaac Newton's late 17th century formulation of the laws of motion and of gravity. We continue to believe that we live in a universe where objects interact. That means our experience of ourselves and our relationships have been dominated by a materialistic view of life that has permeated our culture progressively since the 17th century. Unwittingly, we have become actors on objects or we experience objects acting on us.

In my office, partners often describe their emotional state as the effect of their partner's behavior. This then justifies their emotional response and their interpretations of their partner's intentions. These kinds of conversations in relationships are supported by the Newtonian perspective that has oriented us psychologically to experience ourselves as passive subjects of an objective universe.

Now that quantum physics has offered a much deeper view of how the universe works, it makes sense to question our assumptions and modes of operation that are attached to the materialistic, Newtonian worldview. Up until now, we have suggested this new post-Newtonian science of quantum physics provides a metaphor for our lives, but what if it is more than a metaphor? Since we are energy fields, like all living creatures, would not the laws and dynamics of this fundamental level of existence be applicable to our human lives?

Let's look at the mystery of entangled subatomic particles. Subatomic particles can be entangled, a phenomenon that Einstein called "spooky action at a distance." Science struggles to explain how a photon cut in half or electrons, intimately connected at almost absolute zero temperature, become an entangled pair of subatomic particles. This entanglement allows the pair to have a connection outside of space and time.

If you change the spin of one in the pair, the partner who could be light-years away, will instantaneously change their spin. Science has confirmed this effect but cannot explain it. Entanglement of subatomic particles is the basis for the next breakthrough in quantum computers which will revolutionize computers. Just as in the past, computers advanced from vacuum tubes to transistors to silicon computer chips, and now we will have quantum "entangled" computers.

The entanglement phenomenon emphasizes affinity and connection outside of space-time, not force of action of one object on another. The quantum breakthrough in science opens the door to appreciating ancient wisdom embodied in myth, story, and scriptures. The pre-17th century world was more romantic, more mystical, and more magical about relationships.

"Shot by an arrow," an expression that comes from the Greek story of Eros and Psyche, and the Roman god of desire, Cupid, may turn out to be a realistic approximation of the dynamics of entanglement as well as our own experience of falling in love. We want to show you how wisdom about love was experienced and comprehended before Sir Isaac Newton turned us into material entities and Descartes separated the mind from the body.

QUESTIONS TO PONDER:

- *Think of what attracted you to your partner when you first met.*
- *Do you notice and appreciate those qualities in the present?*

CHAPTER 3

The Real Story of Falling in Love:
FAIRY TALES FOR ADULTS

As I have shared with couples in my therapy practice, understanding quantum mechanics as a metaphor for partner pairing, along with developing relationship skills that teach you to respond to your partner as a wave, can bring breakthroughs in relationships. In the same way, understanding the archetypal characters in fairy tales has helped couples see themselves and shown us how the dynamics of romantic relationships provide the opportunity to grow us through romantic love.

In the metaphor of quantum mechanics, falling in love in the subatomic world is the process where two electrons come to occupy the same orbital space. What makes this possible is the attraction of the electrons and their opposite spins. The opposite spins create a magnetic field that energizes the attraction. This metaphor suggests that there is an affinity to the movement and wave nature of the electrons, and they need to have opposite spins in order to occupy the same orbit.

In the human experience, two individuals who are attracted to each other and establish a partner relationship must also experience similarities with each other and, at the same time, respect and preserve their differences. This is another aspect of the complex dynamics of a successful romantic relationship that is mirrored in the subatomic reality of quantum physics.

In the beginning of the formation of our universe, there were only hydrogen and helium atoms. All electrons were able to occupy the simplest round sphere of the S orbital. After millions of years, stars burned out and exploded and formed complex atoms. These atoms gave electrons and continue to give electrons opportunities for complex orbitals that are illustrated by diagrams in the Appendix, page 184.

The history of electron partners becoming more complex and joining sophisticated molecules that ultimately developed this universe can be seen as a metaphor for how modern life presents more and different complexity for couples as compared to other eras. Our longevity alone makes partnership about more than just survival.

We live beyond our procreation years to an average 80 years as compared to an historical average of 45 years from just a few hundred years ago. This gives couples a greater horizon of purposes in their lives along with more challenges that increase the complexity of the relationship. This opportunity may be the human partners' version of electron pairs moving into more complex orbits.

When an electron moves to a new complex orbit because it has absorbed new energy from a photon, it is uncertain whether the electron partner will join them in the more complex orbit until the reunion occurs. This parallels the distance partners report in psychotherapy after five or ten years of marriage when they describe disconnection, misunderstanding, and conflict. Those five or ten years have developed one or both of them in new ways by virtue of their roles, their new learning or lack of it, and the quality of their self-reflection as a result of these new experiences.

If we want to understand what is involved with ageless love, we can use the process of electron partnering, their disconnection, and reunion to clarify the principles that allow us to stay romantically in love with our partner for a lifetime. The conception that we are material bodies like billiard balls bouncing into each other reduces the meaning of romantic love to an attraction based upon personality, chemicals, hormones, and physical looks where falling and staying in love either works or it does not work, and is out of our control. In this view, we are at the mercy of circumstances.

Let us look at what our western civilization has to say about falling in love before Newton and Descartes and the first scientific revolution changed the way we experience ourselves. The idea of romantic love in western civilization began in the Middle Ages when a knight would choose a woman who was their ideal, and would serve the chosen woman and dedicate his life to taking care of her. However, he would never think of marrying her. Marriage was something you did for having babies and surviving. Marriages in almost all cultures in that era were arranged by parents. Marrying for "love" on a regular basis did not happen until much later in the history of western civilization, and later still in other parts of the world.

The history of romantic love in the West is complex and could fill volumes. The Greeks gave us a vocabulary for love that distinguishes at least four types of love. In practice, the women of Athens in ancient Greece were generally uneducated. There were exceptions, but marrying in that era and subsequent eras was something you did to have babies and acquire a dowry from the bride's father. Common and normative in that period among the educated were homosexual relationships that were deeply engaging because these partnerships consisted of equally educated and developed individuals.

The themes about love from the Jewish Bible range from God's love for his people and their ongoing relationship, to the erotic in *The Song of Songs,* meant as a human as well as spiritual allegory of uniting in love. The Christian Bible develops the theme of love as the self-sacrificing love of a suffering servant who gives his life for others. In these communities, marriage is considered sacred but how this was translated into action is variable.

Passion for both Judaism and Christianity is an aspiration for a higher sphere that is never entirely satiated so that it continues to uplift and transfigure their followers. Later came the troubadours who loved unrequitedly. It was never satiated with physical contact. That was the point. Their lady love was a fountain of inspiration for their heroic activities; it was never intended as a domestic partnership.

While romantic love in our times has been invested with the passion of our religious heritage, we have not been able to construct a popular vision for its potential that comprehends its self-transcending capacity for ongoing personal and spiritual growth. The most popular movies of our era, if they go beyond the initial falling in love stage, often have romantic relationships end in divorce or death.[2] This makes sense if our common experience of romantic relationships diminish and become boring or conflict-ridden domestic arrangements. Who wants to watch that story when it is replaying what we are living at home? The transcendence of love through death is a true experience of transformation, but is that our only vision for the expansion of love in our lives?

Fairy tales have been a part of Western culture for thousands of years. The Grimm brothers were cultural researchers from Germany who, in the early 1800s, collected ancient stories from the oral traditions of western Europe. Some of these stories have their origins in Egypt, Persia, and India. Wandering minstrels would go from town to town and their job was to tell stories to entertain people. These stories were intended for adults, not children. There was no TV or radio so a storyteller coming to town was a big event. The printing press was not available until 1440. Only clergy had access to the Bible and they transmitted those stories by re-telling them to their congregations. We have lived by story.

What we call fairy tales are a part of this story-telling tradition. We have a record of Einstein, one of the fathers of quantum physics, saying that, "If you want your children to be brilliant, read them fairy tales. If you want them to be even more brilliant, read them more fairy tales." Fairy tales, like sacred literature, are part of a tradition that shows us that the physical world that seems so solid can actually be something different. Stories reflect an internal reality of all possibilities that focus on our inner nature and do not limit us to the material conditions of reality.

This perspective is precisely what is presented by quantum mechanics. Quantum science says that the physical world that seems so solid can also be pure potential. In fact, an electron can get to the other side of a wall without going through it. The math proves it.

Fairy tales are stories that have been told and retold and have survived the span of time because they have something of value that is worth re-telling. We share them here as a message from the pre-Newtonian world about their version of wisdom for romantic relationships. Notice the story reflects the internal reality of all possibilities. The characters can behave like a particle or a wave and you see through their dynamics what impacts them and helps them grow into better characters and better partners.

The Princess and The Frog

A perfect example of this is the story of The Princess and the Frog. We all know the synopsis of the Disney version: The Princess kisses the frog and he turns into a prince. In the Grimms version that was told and re-told across Europe from the 1400s to the 1700s, "The Frog King" or "Iron Heinrich," there is no kissing of any frogs. The original story is about how the Princess and the Frog each experience pressure to grow as a result of their relationship. The storyline starts with the young, pre-teen Princess losing her ball and the frog offering to fetch it for her in exchange for visiting her in her home. She agrees because she wants her ball.

Sometime after the frog accomplishes the task, he shows up at her front door to claim the reward for his efforts. The Princess tries to ignore him until her father reminds her it is important to keep her word. The frog lives in the house for a time. Eventually, the frog asks to sleep in the Princess' room. After some time, he asks to sleep in the Princess' bed. The Princess' response is to throw the frog against the wall. This action turns the frog into a handsome prince.

What is this story trying to tell us? We say the frog and the Princess have interacted in such a way that each has transformed their character and benefited tremendously from the relationship. The Princess was counseled by her father to keep her word. She applied his coaching and stretched to fulfill a fundamental ethic of maturity.

The frog was confronted with the Princess' boundaries and learned that she meant it. This transforms the Princess from a girl to a self-responsible woman and the frog from an impulsive creature to a handsome prince. The transformation is made possible because each character changes internally. They each allow themselves to respond to the unfolding events as a wave. The story demonstrates how the characters respond to each other in a way that provides valuable feedback and stimulation for growth. In a sense, we could say that the storyline is about the different realities within each person, evoking different possibilities for response and growth of the characters. Ultimately, there is no objective Princess and objective frog, but rather a potential for re-creation of each character.

I've seen aspects of The Princess and the Frog among couples who are locked in conflict in a conversation because one or the other is either indirect in sharing what they want or overdramatic and blaming their partner for what is missing in the relationship. This can mean a failed conversation if the responding partner takes offense at the initial approach. With a couple who has more skills, the conversation does not have to break down just because it starts on the wrong note. The responding partner has the choice to answer as a wave and ask for clarification or simply ask what behaviors can provide what is missing in the relationship.

This is what quantum physics tells us is true for each of us in our lives. We are not the descriptions we hold of ourselves as absolute qualities that are fixed. Nor are our partners. We may experience our personality or our traumas and make demands around these characteristics or needs, but when we do this, we have become a particle to ourselves and our partner. That doesn't mean we shouldn't ask for accommodations or behaviors that ease our sensitivities. The possibility of being a wave is to work together with our partner and share our vulnerability in such a way that we can help each other heal and grow. This takes skills. This also stabs at the assumption that the world somehow exists objectively outside of us.

Psychotherapy has understood this dynamic to different degrees by ascribing strong emotions and interpretations of people and events as representing subjective feelings from previous experiences that are projected onto others, thus making it difficult to resolve relationship issues. Projection highlights how skewed we are in our interpretations of reality. This is how quantum physics challenges our self-understanding. The new science invites us to be both humble about what we think we know of ourselves and each other and, at the same time, invites us to become powerful by engaging in the creative engagement in possibility as a wave.

This is the philosophical framework behind learning new skills that do not particle-ize ourselves and our partner. We need to learn how to share our vulnerable selves and ask for the changes in behavior that support our emotional well-being. This is only possible when we step away from the interpretations that materialize ourselves and our partner and imply that they are who they are, and we are who we are. This traps us in hurt, disillusionment, and no solution. This disallows possibility and erodes trust and connection.

In short, we need to learn how to become waves. We need to learn our perceptions may not be the reality we think they are. We need to learn behavioral skills that keep us from becoming defensive and attacking others. When there is a conflict, we need to know there is valuable learning embedded in the issue that can move us forward as a partnership, if we allow it.

Let's consider a couple in a conflict that may appear at first glance as a minor issue. A wife complained that she was not included in her husband's company holiday dinner because his siblings do not approve of extended family joining the event. She was angry that her husband was not standing up for her and asserting his leadership role in the family business. Their arguments were fiery and protracted. She felt disrespected and excluded and believed it was appropriate for her to participate as the wife of the president of the company. Underneath, she felt hurt, excluded and misunderstood by her husband. At the same time, the husband felt disrespected and pressured by his wife in a role that was new to him.

Eventually with wave listening, each partner saw their role in the conflict and heard something new. The wife saw that her complaining was not productive and stopped. She was able to express her hurt without blame or anger. The husband could now hear her. He also began to see that he needed to step out of his comfort zone and assert his leadership in the business. He was raised as the oldest child to be responsible for his siblings' feelings. He now saw this as a handicap in making good business decisions. He started with small steps that eventually created boundaries with his siblings and limited their influence to their defined roles in the company.

This was not an easy issue to resolve. Each partner was determined that the other was unreasonable and unlikeable. It took months to find a solution to the conversation. In the end, the wife felt accomplished that she stood up for herself and won her husband's primary loyalty over his siblings' pressure. She felt important again to her husband and important to herself. This was a significant step forward for her own development and the growth of the marital partnership.

The husband, for his part, eventually saw that he was hamstrung by his desire to please his siblings and his fear of displeasing them. He realized that he needed to assert himself because his vision of the business was different from theirs, and to navigate the business he needed to accept the responsibility of his role. This gave him the will to step into the full leadership of his company as his father had designed for him.

What began as a conflict initiated by the wife's perception of hurt that then aggravated the relationship for close to a year became the opportunity for important development for each partner. The wife stepped into respectful self-assertion by internally claiming her partnership with her husband and by speaking effectively in their conversation. The husband, on his part, stepped out of the role he had learned in his family to accommodate his siblings' feelings, and stepped into the new challenge of steering a business that needed his independent judgment for good decision-making. This was a developmental win for both partners and a huge leap forward for the partnership.

This is how the push and pull of ordinary life can yield big rewards when couples bring their honest feelings and share them productively. A small matter can create new opportunities to express feelings and seek new behaviors that cause realignments in the structure of your partnership, your relationship to work, and your experience of yourself. Notice too, it is a win for both partners. Your romantic partnership is a continuous source for learning, provided you know how to speak with each other in a way that works for both of you.

Cinderella

Let's look at another story that Disney fractured by rewriting it in the Newtonian worldview: Cinderella. We all know the story: Cinderella cries and her fairy godmother comes to the rescue. She goes to the ball, and at midnight runs home, dropping her slipper along the way. The prince falls in love with her and seeks her, while she waits passively.

In the Grimm Brothers' version that predates Newton, Cinderella forcefully requests permission to go to the ball. Instead, her stepmother gives her the impossible task (a theme that will appear again in Psyche's story which follows), of separating lentils from ashes which she accomplishes with the help of pigeons and turtle doves, birds that partner for life. Still, her stepmother will not let her go. Cinderella responds by taking matters into her own hands and sews her own dress for the ball. She is not passive. But her stepsisters tear the dress and ridicule Cinderella for thinking she is worthy of attending the ball.

Cinderella prays at her mother's grave and as she cries, a hazel tree grows above the gravesite and birds magically drop her a dress.

She walks to the ball during the day, dances with the prince, and he falls in love with her. At dusk she runs home. Dusk is the time when the masculine sun diminishes and the feminine moon comes to prominence. A woman can function in the masculine world, but she also wants her man to join her in the feminine world.

The prince follows her and tries to catch her while she hides in a pigeon house near her home and she escapes. The next day, Cinderella repeats her actions: She goes to the ball, dances with the prince and suddenly leaves at dusk. She climbs into a pear tree near her home, escaping into the house before the prince can find her in the pear tree. Cinderella is behaving like a bird, requiring her man to pursue her to appreciate the feminine qualities that are so delicate.

On the third day, Cinderella dances all day with the prince and again runs home at dusk. This time, however, the prince is ready for her escape. He uses his intelligence, gentleness, and discrimination to find her. He puts sticky pitch on the stairs to catch her shoe, just as he would catch a bird with sticky glue. The prince declares that to whomever this slipper belongs, he will marry. Then he goes to Cinderella's home, which he strategically believes to be near the pear tree and pigeon house, and after the two stepsisters "cosmetically" cut their feet to try to fit into the shoe, the prince eventually finds Cinderella, and declares, "This is my wife."

Note that the prince actively seeks Cinderella, even as Cinderella is active in pursuing her life goals. She goes to the prince's party three times, but does not fawn on him the first, second, or even the third time; she never says, "I want you." Rather, she requires the prince to actively pursue her to show that he is worthy of capturing her heart. She needs to know he really wants her and waits for him to take action. Both play an active part in this process.

In addition, the symbolism of the birds has meaning. They represent the soul, which can fly with joy, happiness, and love. When Cinderella prays and cries at her mother's grave, her tears allow a magical tree to grow. The magical birds that live in the tree bring her a dress from above. Later we will consider how meditation and prayer offers us a connection to the creative energy of the quantum dimension of life.

Cinderella is an active participant in the creation of her dress. The dress represents a gift from the spiritual world, inspired by her love for her deceased mother, not from some random fairy godmother. Cinderella's birdlike behavior, of hiding in the pear tree and pigeon house, expresses her soul's freedom and sense of worth as she pursues her desires.

The Cinderella of the Brothers Grimm represents a more defined personality than the Disney version. The Grimms capture Cinderella's sense of self and self-worth. She connects spiritually to her mother and the world of soul freedom as in the symbolism of birds. She wants love in her life with a man whom she knows will also want her. Her vision for herself forms a foundation for deep partnership.

By her actions, Cinderella makes it clear she operates in a higher energy orbit and is looking to join with a partner who matches her energy. At the same time, the story makes clear the contrast of her feminine resourcefulness with the masculine strategies of the prince. In quantum terms, they are electrons with opposite spins preparing to share an orbit.

How we experience falling in love gives us insight into how to maintain the falling in love experience. The story of Cinderella highlights the distinction of each partner's personalities along with the chemistry of their connection. Cinderella portrays an independent woman who knows what she wants and takes responsibility for creating it, and the Prince matches her with his own energy and creativity. The dynamics of the story offers the best dating advice! How they negotiate partnership in their marriage, we will never know. What women do for love is often to surrender themselves. The story of Eros and Psyche picks up where Cinderella's leaves off.

Psyche and Eros

In our Western tradition there is one dramatic example of falling in love forever between the gods. This 2000-year old myth clearly demonstrates the complexity of falling in love and staying in love forever. We have written in another book, *The Marriage Map*, about this mythical story that comes from ancient Greece that develops the journey of two lovers where their love transforms their lives and their relationship. The development of Psyche and Eros' personalities, and the conflicts they endure as individuals and as a couple, match precisely the challenges and opportunities we believe are available now to human individuals in their romantic partnerships. We can learn much from this ancient wisdom.

Psyche is the only goddess who gave up her goddess-hood to become a human being and enjoy a human experience. However, she was so beautiful no one would marry her. The goddess of love, Aphrodite, became jealous of her beauty.

Aphrodite tells her son Eros (also known as Cupid) to shoot an arrow into Psyche so she will fall in love with a monster and get rid of Psyche. When Eros is about to shoot the arrow, he is startled by how beautiful Psyche is, and he cuts his own finger on the arrow and this causes him to fall in love with Psyche. He brings Psyche back to his heavenly mansion, but he insists that Psyche never see his face other than the middle of the night when it is pitch dark. This is a metaphor for the unconscious relationship that many couples experience after marrying, especially if they marry young, before they know who they are.

Eros and Psyche marry against his mother's wishes. Psyche first accommodates her new husband and agrees to live in the mountains and never see his face in the light. This works for a time, but her curiosity and worry that he might be a demon, as Psyche's sisters suggest, cause her to sneak a look at him in the middle of the night with a candle while he sleeps. She is so startled by how beautiful Eros is that her hand trembles and some of the oil from the candle drips on Eros and wakes him up.

Upon seeing that Psyche broke their agreement, the angered Eros goes back to the heavenly realms to be with his mother and leaves Psyche.

His point of view is certainly understandable as he feels betrayed that Psyche broke her promise that provided for his privacy.

Psyche's perspective is also authentic and familiar to the female pattern where the woman begins by accommodating in her relationship and then regrets her accommodation. It also reflects the inevitable feminine desire for connection and emotional intimacy with a husband for which he is unprepared.

For Eros' part, he comes across as any man in our era who is averse to emotional intimacy, at least at first, and who withdraws. Moreover, Eros takes refuge in his mother's abode in heaven which offers a safe space for withdrawing from dealing with his emotional pain. Here, both partners reveal their immaturity.

This segment of the story is rich in details that represent both wave/particle phenomena as well as the beginning of a developmental transition. Later we will discuss how both of these dynamics overlap and point to the essential dynamics of growing the heart and mind over a lifetime.

Back to our story, Psyche is unhappy with the relationship agreement she has made. She feels stifled and bored and afraid that her husband may be a demon. Her lack of development and her fear come together to contract her behavior like a particle, and she projects a particle interpretation onto her husband.

Notice that Psyche does not start a conversation with her husband about her new feelings and needs and what new behaviors would make her happy. She conjures up a strategy that ultimately burns Eros with hot wax. No wonder he leaves; he has been assaulted with distrust. For Eros' part, he does not know how to listen and understand the underlying feelings that motivate Psyche's impulsive behavior. They are both trapped in a relationship they have outgrown and need to transition from a traditional and un-reflected "we" relationship to a personalized relationship consisting of two individuals who negotiate their needs and become partners in life.

At this point of the story, Psyche intuitively knows she must grow. This is where Psyche stretches by finding courage to activate her mind to focus on her goals and discipline her heart so she doesn't get overwhelmed by her emotions and act out her feelings. These are steps of growth that are needed to fulfill her part of the partnership so she can communicate effectively, and focus on what is important to her in the relationship. This represents the development of the mind.

How does this ancient story show us how Psyche grows? Psyche goes on a series of seemingly impossible trials by which Aphrodite intends to cause Psyche to fail in order to keep her son, Eros, separated from Psyche. But ultimately Psyche responds to Aphrodite's ordeals and develops in ways that builds her ability to be an independent self: conquering her emotions and balancing her desire to care for others with her desire to accomplish; learning to deal with masculine energy without confronting it.

In her final trial to reconnect with Eros, Psyche travels to the underworld, controls her speech, resists temptations and distractions from her purpose, and successfully retrieves a special beauty cream that Aphrodite requires. When Psyche sees how disheveled she looks as she prepares to see Eros, she decides to put some of the goddess cream on her face. Immediately she dies as she is still human.

Eros sees from the distance of his heavenly realm the spectacular courage of Psyche's accomplishments and who she has become that he cannot resist loving her and re-joining her in partnership. He comes down from the heavens and lifts her dead body and brings her to his father, Zeus, and pleads for her life. In dying, Psyche inspires Eros to separate appropriately from his mother and develop his individuality, just as Psyche's love for Eros inspired her to develop herself.

Romantic love invites the challenge of creating and recreating love over the lifetime of a committed relationship. The pre-Newtonian world understood this, at least mythologically. In Psyche's story, she steps out of the initial agreement of the relationship and wants more from Eros, though she does not know how to invite what she wants. He retreats to be with his mother because he is unable to respond to the level of intimacy that Psyche wants, and does not know how to explore with

Psyche the meaning of her offensive behavior. They each came to the end of what their development allowed. Their disengagement is the natural result of becoming particles with each other. Neither had the skills to be present for their partner and listen as a wave.

It is Psyche's love for Eros and her perseverance that inspires her journey into the underworld, and the tasks she accomplishes grow her as an individual. Her development then inspires Eros to stretch into his independence by separating from his mom and claiming his wife, not just because she is a beautiful woman, but for how she has inspired him and drawn him close to her with the growth of her inner self.

Psyche's journey gains her a new self-discipline and strategic thinking for solving obstacles. This maturity gives her a more sophisticated individuality that suggests the accomplishment of a new, more complex orbit.

Eros and Psyche's separation highlights both the dynamics of mystery and predictability as well as the tumultuous transition that particle behavior can cause. Psyche had accommodated Eros' requirements for privacy in the relationship but, after some time, she found herself lonely. There was too much emotional distance for her and not enough emotional connection. Psyche could not find an effective individual voice to express her loneliness because she did not know how. Her intrusive behavior to use a candle to unveil who Eros really was, effectively treated Eros as a particle to be exposed. This collapsed the trust in the relationship that is necessary for the partners to see and respect each other. This caused a breach in the relationship that made further development imperative.

Psyche's commitment to grow herself gains her new internal strengths, and adds a new level of self-definition and complexity to the relationship. This is how Psyche re-creates the mystery in her marriage. This is an ideal outcome, and perhaps the reason why the story has lasted so long in our culture. We say that Psyche and Eros' disconnection is a very common experience for romantic partnerships after five or 10 years of being together. One or both partners change and see the world from a different perspective and want new experiences in their relationship.

The story of Eros and Psyche is an engaging story that could be any couple's story of transforming their relationship to a more complex partnership of two individuated personalities. It is also a story that parallels what happens when one partner in an electron pairing experiences the pressure along with new energy and goes through the process of becoming available for a more complex orbit.

This remarkable tale foreshadows, in our view, the dynamics of contemporary romantic relationships and the opportunities for continuous self and relationship transformation. This is made possible by partners who aspire to be equally dynamic and take on the challenge of their individual, ongoing development, and the creative potential of their partnership.

We are proposing that a developmental accomplishment in humans is akin to electrons gaining new energy and moving to a more complex orbit. The new capacity to create and enjoy a more complex life at a new developmental level approximates in human terms the quantum leap that electrons experience when they move from simple atoms like helium and hydrogen to more complex atoms like oxygen and carbon. Nature has orbits of increasing complexity (See Appendix: Electron orbitals). It should be no surprise that human nature has orbits of increasing complexity.

For humans, it is dramatic and unsettling when one partner shifts into a more complex level of self-awareness and purpose. It is a rough transition for the individual as well as for the partner because it interferes with their familiar connection and creates uncomfortable distance. This is commonly where human partners come to marriage counseling or end their relationship because they do not know how to bridge the painful gap. The ability to talk about how this feels and what each partner wants for their future is critical to laying out the path to an upgraded partnership. The motivation of the left-behind partner to grow is another key requirement for the partners to rejoin their union on a new level.

The development of two individuated partners can be fragile because equal partnership can become a power struggle. Again, this is where skills in sharing, listening, and negotiating are critical. The pioneering partner who upgraded first, needs to encourage and emotionally support without reinforcing dependency. This usually involves another new stretch of development for the individuated partner, this time for the heart, in empathy skills. This is how partnership stimulates ongoing development.

The equality of men and women in our era also allows us to further personalize the metaphor of electrons who occupy orbits together because they have equal energies along with different spins. As we learn about the developmental transformations that are possible in adult life that occur for men and women at similar or different times depending on our life journey, we can also identify with how gaining new development, or in electron terms, new energy, may cause an electron or a partner to become distant (or join a new orbit) for a while.

It took me, Barbara, 10 years of marriage to begin to move from the initial Psyche phase of an "unconscious" or "belonging" relationship towards the phase of conscious partnership. By the time I was 30 years old, I felt disconnected from Michael as he was growing through his experience as a boss and leader in creating and managing a new medical practice and interacting with his office staff in a very intense way. I felt left out and rather overwhelmed with being a parent of two girls where my mothering role consisted mostly of empathy and support. Feeling left out of partnership and not as developed in my individual life pushed me to grow myself and seek a more equal relationship with Michael.

I went back to school to complete my Ph.D. and define myself and my competence more clearly. This is a parallel of the description of Psyche as she moved into her independence to become an equal to Eros. Michael responded to my new way of being by stretching to meet my desire for a deeper, emotional connection. For Michael, this pushed him to resolve an underlying resentment towards what he perceived as his mom's harsh criticism and forgive her. His memories of his mom's anger intensified his experience of my anger and made it impossible for him to hear me. On my side, I needed to learn how to express my vulnerability by sharing the fear and hurt from my childhood about feeling abandoned by my father that was underneath my anger about feeling left out of his new life as a boss. This opened the door for Michael to let go of his childhood hurt, expand the capacity of his heart, and hear me as an equal partner asking respectfully for his attention.

The growth of our personalities over time echoes the Greek story of Psyche, as well as the Brothers Grimm stories where characters are transformed by the dynamics of their relationships. These mythological characters, like us in our era, are not unchangeable material personalities. We add our experience and voice to their theme that romantic relationships stimulate and invite us to develop ourselves and match the energy and complexity of our partner in the orbit that connects us to the deepest chain of life.

QUESTIONS TO PONDER:

- *How have you and your partner changed over time since you first fell in love?*
- *Do you feel a deeper connection to your partner, or not?*
- *Do you feel more of a need for independence or belonging?*
- *Do you feel a deeper sense of purpose or a lack of enthusiasm?*

CHAPTER 4

Turning up the Romance: Partners Are Different

In quantum mechanics we described how two electrons can share an orbit as a wave, but only if they have opposite spins. Electrons would normally repel each other as they have a negative charge but they can, according to the Pauli Exclusion Principle, share an orbit if they have opposite spins. This is a strong analogy for the romantic relationship that allows two romantic partners to move in the same orbit as waves and it is their opposite spins that allow this to happen.

To fall in love forever with your romantic partner, it is critical to understand and accept the differences between you and your partner. After all, this is what attracted you to each other in the first place. Understanding the differences between you and your partner is one path that can lead to more romance in your marriage because treating your partner in the same way you want to be treated yourself typically leads to less romance and less passion.

Understanding Our Differences

There are many ways to talk about our differences. We may have different temperaments. We certainly have different family and personal histories. Whether we are the only child or one of two, three or more siblings provides unique experiences of connection. If we were raised with a father in the home or not is another dynamic that affects our perception of relationship. Did our parents work together in their parenting? All these and more aspects of our history reflects a different experience of relationship.

Recent cultural trends suggest that men and women are essentially the same except for obvious biological differences. At the same time, newer technology such as brain scans has revealed great differences between the ways that the male and female brain functions. We know that women can go back and forth between the hemispheres more quickly. We also know that sex hormones have a profound effect on the developing brain structures of children. About 80 percent of men and women exhibit those differences. There is, however, a significant minority of men and women who exhibit some neurological characteristics more typical of the opposite sex.

The value of anticipating and appreciating these generalized differences between men and women's brains is that it invites you to distinguish and accept your partner as different in whatever way they are different. At the same time, it moves you into an arena of personal development because it will put pressure on you to learn, respect, and contend with someone who is different from yourself. This will allow you, if you are willing, to become a better lover.

The complexities of marriage include the dynamics of two different styles of brain functioning, yet each partner in a married couple often treats the other as if they both have the same kind of brain. This leads to presenting arguments to convince your partner you are right as if there is only one "right" in a conversation. The art of being happily married encompasses understanding our similarities as human beings, our differences as individuals, and our differences as men and women.

It remains for each partnership to define their respective roles. In a romantic relationship it is critical to accept and appreciate the differences between you. That is what attracted you to your partner.

Over time, what makes your partner happy will change. Learning what behaviors are now making your partner happy and feeling loved and updating your partner with your own self-discovery is a very important learning process. Practicing these relationship skills will deepen your connection with each other and contribute to the healing and integration of both partners' personalities.

QUESTION TO PONDER:

- *What are the differences you notice in yourself and your partner in terms of your values, your temperaments, and family backgrounds?*

CHAPTER 5

Inevitable Quantum Jumps in Our Romantic Relationships
STAGES OF ADULT DEVELOPMENT

There are inevitable changes that occur throughout an adult lifetime that will destabilize your world, stress your relationships, cause you to reformulate your philosophy of life, and possibly even alter the direction of your work. These changes start gradually and may become uncomfortable if not resolved. These changes may also grow into more comprehensive shifts of points of view about who you are as an individual.

These more dramatic shifts are not guaranteed; they are a function of development that occurs because you or your partner have grown through competence at work, or in a mentor relationship, or an experience of leadership of some kind, in the family or community. This holistic growth of point of view represents a structural developmental stage change. It occurs because your life experience has stretched you beyond your familiar thinking and feeling framework and the resulting disorganization challenges you to find a new framework and at a more inclusive level that makes sense of your life. It is not unlike the quantum jump physicists describe when electrons transition to a new, higher energy orbit. We are prepared to tell you what to expect and how to navigate these transitions so that you and everyone around you will benefit.

The Role of the Human Brain in Creating Our Experiences

Albert Einstein and Niels Bohr, both great scientists in the early 1900s, were among the first to observe that as an electron gains energy when it rotates around the nucleus, it does not gradually expand its orbit. Rather it absorbs energy (photons) and does what is called a quantum jump in physics. This means it suddenly moves from one orbit to a much bigger, more complex orbit when the energy increases. This jump is required as the mathematics of the orbit can only harmoniously exist if it moves to the next quantum level.

We can understand this like a string on a violin. To have a harmonious sound you need to move from one note to another. Note that the "in-between" sound will decay and disintegrate very quickly. The orbit of electrons can only move in these quantum jumps. There are no in-between options for electrons. In our human lifetime there are quantum leaps in our consciousness that occur over a lifecycle.

This is a metaphor for the possibilities of our development through the stimulation and challenge of ageless love. Inevitably, the field of love we live in will change over time as we human beings go through quantum jumps of consciousness. These movements from a low-energy orbit to a higher energy orbit is uncomfortable for both partners. This is where skills in sharing and creating understanding about new feelings, perceptions and needs are important for both partners.

For humans, these jumps are not experienced subjectively as an immediate transformation like it appears to occur for an electron. Of course, we do not know the internal experience of an electron for a comparison. For humans, the stage shifts gradually, building tension between two perspectives until it resolves in favor of the new stage.

For a period of time an individual can feel stuck in between two levels which is unsettling. When you do settle into the new, more complex level of human consciousness, you feel much more stable. However, this change can create tension with your romantic partner.

Every human being goes through life changes like an electron where there are shifts in the experience of self that are equivalent to quantum jumps. With each "jump" in awareness of ourselves in relation to the world, we move to a more developed stage of "self." In addition to increasing complexity, each successive stage change alternates the emphasis in its movement of feeling close to those we love, to feeling more separate and autonomous from those we love. It is a back-and-forth development over a lifespan that alternates the locus of development with the heart or the mind. Feeling close represents an emphasis on developing empathy and connection, and the mind represents an emphasis on reflective thinking. Each succeeding stage adds nuances to the subtleties of feeling and thinking.

We have already applied a developmental perspective to the story of Psyche and Eros. It is worth abstracting the concepts of these stages and going into some details about these qualitative developmental changes that are associated with aging but are not guaranteed by virtue of time.

The kind of development that is predictable and based on biology is a quantitative development where you age into a new chapter of your life because your life circumstances have changed simply because you are older. The premier psychologist associated with this quantitative view of psychological development is Erik Erikson.

The development we are talking about that approximates the quantum changes in electrons is a different schema for development. This model is based on cognitive and emotional accomplishment. This is a different view of the maturing process that distinguishes the quality of perception, analytical and moral thinking, locus of authority, and other parameters of perspective taking. It is a comprehensive view of what is possible in adult development and it is associated with psychologists such as Jean Piaget, Lawrence Kohlberg, Robert Kegan, and others.

Together and separately, these psychologists have contributed qualitative maps for how adults accomplish stage changes over the course of their adult years. These developmental changes are significant because they represent meaningful shifts in the experience of being an individual. Each stage change involves a transformation that many adults accomplish depending on numerous factors such as their engagement in life and, to some degree, their intellectual and emotional capacity to digest and personalize a new framework.

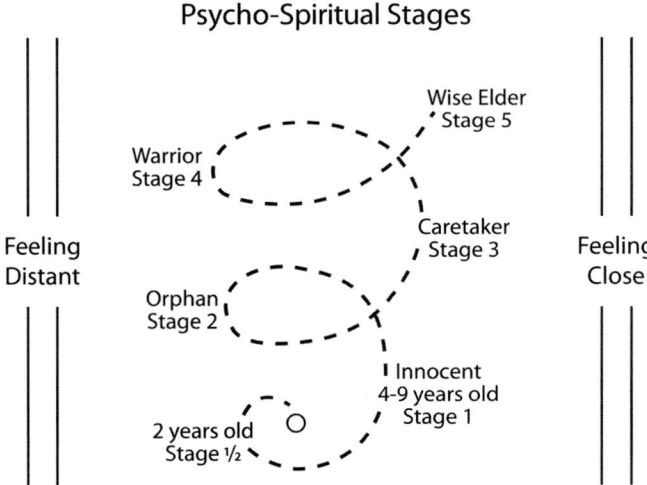

This is a picture of the spiral of the stages of personal development that represent quantum jumps in our experience of being a "self." We start out as a newborn sucking on mother's breast and feeling complete unity with the breast.

At the age of about two, we have taken a step towards feeling separate from mother and we start saying "No!" and feel adamant about having things our way. This represents a move to the side of autonomy. We feel we "are" our immediate needs and physical impulses. Logic is not yet a part of our awareness.

As we become ages five through nine, we move back towards the side of feeling close to those we love and we are so happy to be part of a family. We begin to use logic and respond to rules, and we want to please our parents. We also want to please our teachers. This is Stage 1.

In our teens, we again feel more autonomous and separate from those we love, and we want things our way. We are not so concerned about pleasing our parents. We value our desires and wishes, and this defines our sense of "self." We start taking seriously the journey to define our own identity. This is Stage 2.

The fairytale about the Princess and the Frog alludes to this passage in the teen years. It is a description of each character's movement from impulsiveness to the very early beginnings of understanding the mutuality of relationship that is a Stage 3 accomplishment. It is psychology before there was psychology because it is a story that helps young people understand the transformation they are going through. These stories are considered archetypal for this reason and have endured for centuries because they are maps for the path of personal development. The Princess pledged a home visit with a stranger frog without thinking about the consequences, and the frog made bold sexual advances without any cue that it was welcome. These characters learn new behaviors and life lessons as the listener of the story learns with them.

Both the frog and the Princess are starting to understand the very basics about relationships: caring about others' feelings and responsible and socially acceptable behavior. The Princess learns she has to keep her word and the frog learns he needs to have a respect for the needs and boundaries of others. This is a good beginning but they have a ways to go. They are not ready for a relationship that is a partnership. These stage accomplishments are not a small project and the growth to Stage 3 is a huge achievement for individuals and for society.

The 20s or early 30s is ideally a time to commit to a partnership relationship and start a family. This is an accomplishment of maturity. In Stage 3, we feel emotionally attached to the responsibility for loving and taking care of our own family. Our "self" is no longer experienced as our needs and wishes and desires. Rather we now experience our "self" as a "we" because we "are" our relationships. We experience we "have" needs and desires and wishes, but they take a back seat to our focus on the special people who are our family. We call this the Caregiver stage.

In Stage 3, the Caretaker stage, relationships become more intimate to us than our own individual needs, desires and wishes. Not everybody gets here. There are a lot of people with adult bodies who do not attain this level of responsibility and care for others. Typically, the reason has something to do with addictions like substance abuse that derail the focus on taking responsibility for goals that create an adult life. Stage 3 represents a caring partner, family member, and good citizen. It is a very satisfying and successful stage of accomplishment.

The story of Cinderella portrays two characters who have the confidence to pursue their goals. Both Cinderella and the Prince's behavior is socially appropriate and respectful of each other and themselves. This is a more integrated sense of taking responsibility and appreciating that one's own interests must be in agreement with another for a relationship to go forward. This is Stage 3.

A stage change that causes more closeness to those you love represents an emphasis on the growth of the heart: deeper empathy, an enhanced valuing of connection, and more refined feelings. The stages that create the experience of more distance in relationships emphasize the development of the mind and this growth provides for more complex thinking. Note that starting at Stage 3, the first adult stage, more development does not necessarily mean a better person. Future development beyond Stage 3 depends upon the motivation of the individual and the opportunity for exposure to mentors or challenging projects that push us to develop our talents or interests. In our 30s and early 40s, we may begin to feel that we need a more satisfying career where we express our unique talents, as well as personal time to focus on our own interests.

Once again, we feel separate from those we love because our focus is our self-expression. However, our sense of "self" is expanded. We now experience that we no longer "are" our relationships, rather, we "have" relationships. We can work on our relationships to solve problems and negotiate our needs. In this Stage 4, what we identify as our sense of "self" is our beliefs, principles and values. This is a stage of individuation that can lead to a conscious partnership that has a quality of being designed by the partners themselves.

The first enhancement from the Stage 3 caregiver to the Stage 4 warrior is a project for the mind and it provides a new quality of self-understanding and strategic thinking. In the mythological story of Psyche and Eros we see the movement of Psyche's maturity from Stage 3 to Stage 4. Psyche accomplishes important growth: she learns to control her feelings, deal effectively with male emotions, control her speech, focus on accomplishing goals, and she achieves remarkable self-discipline and strategic thinking for solving problems. This prepares her for partnership.

Eros also grows from being satisfied with a relationship where he is totally in control to a relationship of equals. This requires him to leave the protection of his mother, Aphrodite, and acknowledge Psyche as his equal partner. The journey to this accomplishment for Eros and Psyche's marriage includes a separation for a while as the relationship experienced a rupture when each partner needed to focus on their own development before they could recreate their marriage at a new level.

The growth to Stage 4, the Warrior stage, destabilizes a marriage when one partner advances to this new stage and the other stays behind. If only one partner advances to this individuated stage, this imbalance inevitably becomes a disturbance to the intimacy of the relationship. During the transition, the person is conflicted and confused as to their own values. Their values are changing. Moreover, because the partners are no longer attending to the same interests and values, conversation is harder. There is misunderstanding or no understanding. Predictably, one form of this imbalance occurs when one partner is the domestic partner and the other partner has a complex job that involves intellectual stretching as well as leadership responsibility.

There is nothing that prepares a couple for this tension and confusion. This is when the partners need new skills and coaching to understand and respond adequately to the challenge of re-creating their relationship. This involves, at the very least, expressing themselves and listening at a completely new level of presence and self-expression.

As an example, I recall a couple who came to see me about a conflict that arose after eight years of marriage. The husband no longer was willing to participate in weekly extended family gatherings as he had for years. This is an example of an unexpected redirection of energy and values by one partner that produced a rupture in the partnership connection.

The wife responded with confusion and anger. Our work consisted in helping them both understand that the husband's so-called rebellion was not selfish or mean-spirited but rather a new need for personal time to relax and read, or pursue a hobby. The sessions helped this couple express their deeper feelings and negotiate a family schedule that worked for both of them.

It was hard for the wife to understand. To her, this was tantamount to rebellion. She was coming from a Stage 3 belonging perspective and her husband was developing a more Stage 4 individuated point of view. If you have not faced this conflict, you might make light of this, but changing the agreements about how you share togetherness in your relationship after years of agreement to do it a certain way, and then the agreement is challenged, is not easy. It is a stretch for the relationship.

There are other variations in individual development that can disturb the connection between partners. If both partners work and either choose not to have children or have helpers with their young children, both are on the same professional track which sounds easier, but it does not avoid tension and the challenge of growing as a couple. It is a different challenge. Two partners who are focused on accomplishment are likely to be very independent, strategic, and in their heads. This often leads a couple towards a power struggle where their independent competence generates conversations about who is right.

This qualitative understanding of development over a lifetime sees a movement from connectedness in childhood to autonomy in the teen years, and again connectedness when you marry and create a family, and then differentiation as one partner works and becomes more independent while the other is a caregiver and more connection oriented. Each changing developmental circumstance will predictably alter the relationship as the partners shift their focus over time towards and away from the partnership. The couple needs to enrich their conversations with deeper sharing and upgrade their skills to negotiate how to stay connected.

Stage development is very individual. It occurs because there are new experiences, new challenges that cause new growth. When one partner accomplishes the warrior upgrade before the other, it is a profound disruption to their connection. We talk about this in our *Falling in Love Forever* marriage classes so that our couples can understand what they are no doubt experiencing. It reduces the stress to know that they can build a bridge by learning how to talk together. Eventually, the second partner will be enriched in their development if they choose to grow.

The challenge of individuated development when both partners have accomplished this at the same time is parallel individuation. It brings a couple into conflict and competition that can be unpleasant and divisive. This puts pressure on the couple to stretch beyond this stage. While this individuated stage often comes at a time when most people are raising older children, it is not a stage that emphasizes connection. It is more about solving problems, creating procedures, accomplishing, and ideology.

What is next for this couple's development, if they are willing, is learning how to listen with an open heart. Listening at this new level brings them emotional growth that enriches them as individuals and as a partnership. This kind of couple gets a boost in the direction of balancing individuality with a much deeper connection. This is a remarkable achievement that ultimately can lead to a profound level of wisdom if these individuals continue growing over time. In navigating these developmental transitions, the commitment to developing oneself and learning skills to share one's ongoing, evolving self is a key to ageless love. It also illuminates the developmental value of romantic partnership.

The next development to Stage 5, what we call the wise elder stage, is a stretch for the heart to grow and integrate with the mind. This provides a new capacity for empathizing with another without losing self. It is a remarkable achievement to grow as an individual and a relationship over a lifetime. The desire for emotional closeness with a partner as an expansion to a well-defined self is what creates a momentum for this new quality of relationship and this enhancement to self-development. In this way, the romantic partnership itself is the catalyst for growth. The promise of *Ageless Love* is fulfilled when partners come to their relationship with motivation for self-discovery along with mutual respect and a willingness to collaborate and continuously grow to create love.

Stage 5 is an opportunity that becomes available in the later years when we get to our 50s and 60s, to feel an enhanced connection to those we love: our partner, our adult children and grandchildren, and the human family. We are less preoccupied with our own personal need for independence. We now experience that we have beliefs, principles and values, but we are not our beliefs. Our beliefs are not our identity. We can refine our beliefs, work on them, and we can accept other people more easily who have different beliefs, principles, and values.

We experience ourselves as a quality of being, a "self" independent of our circumstances, and independent of our values and principles. Our "self" is bigger than any specific set of values. We are on our way to a more spiritual identity, a connection with Being itself. It is called the Wise Elder stage because these individuals represent a remarkable level of personal integration and contribution to the people in their lives.

Notice the mind and the heart alternate as the leading focus of development over the lifespan until the heart and mind come together and integrate their development in the wise elder stage. This occurs no sooner than the fifth decade of life. There are a lot of important life experiences that occur before then and the challenges of those life experiences are the raw material that can stretch and grow us and open us to an increasingly complex capacity to engage in life. Our romantic relationship is a key source for challenge and stimulus that catalyzes this development.

The exact timetable for these developmental changes may vary depending on our gender or what age we marry and start a family. When we transition and experience a quantum jump in our consciousness, it is generally not a smooth process. The movement from the caretaker stage to the warrior stage creates complexities for the partner who is moving to the new stage as well as for their partner. When you are accustomed to your partner being a team player and focusing on the family relationship, it is difficult to accept your partner's new way of being in the world.

The difference between the couples who move through this time of chaos productively, and those who don't, are individuals who realize they need skills to grow and understand themselves and their partner more deeply. Their movement to a deeper connection requires that they each express themselves more authentically and take responsibility for the quality of their connection consciously. This takes time and humility, and living as a wave, not as a particle. For many couples, this is a learning process that requires psychotherapy or an equivalent program of self-development where both partners participate.

We bring this concept of stage growth to your attention because it is useful in itself to understand the evolution of your experience of self as an individual over time and how it impacts your relationship. Without this knowledge, it would be easy to conclude when you experience a transition in stages that, as a relationship, you have "grown apart." This observation is accurate; it certainly describes how it feels. How you understand what you are going through makes all the difference in reconnecting and maximizing your future growth as individuals and as a partnership.

We also want to draw a parallel between electron and human pairs that disconnect from their partners for a while. In the language of physics, electrons acquire new energy. For human partners, they individuate which can be understood metaphorically as acquiring a new perspective that renews and re-orients their energy. Both sets of partners, electrons and humans, disconnect from their relationship orbit for a while. Leaving the orbit for humans can occur under the same roof as well as physical separation.

The parallel with quantum physics provides us with an understanding and reassurance that these dynamics of growth and change are normal, predictable, and meant for meaningful development over a lifetime. These transitions certainly challenge a couple, and there are pathways to re-create connection. Bridging a developmental gap is one of the themes in our *Falling in Love Forever* relationship course for couples because it is a dilemma that must be understood properly to restore respect and communication.

QUESTION TO PONDER:

- *Have you and your partner moved into different stages over the years? Share these thoughts with your partner.*

CHAPTER 6

The Mystery of the Divided Brain

*U*p until now we have been describing the dynamics of developing the heart and the mind. At different age intervals, assuming there are life challenges and an intention to respond to them and stretch, the mind develops new and more refined ways of thinking, creating, and interpreting experience. Likewise, at other times through other challenges, more refined feelings become available for experience and understanding. These new experiences eventually stabilize and form new structures of thinking and feeling that can be distinguished as stages.

The developmental stage concept can be applied without scoring in a therapeutic setting if the therapist is well informed of the complex criteria that determines each stage. The concepts of stage development have also been utilized for cultural reflection, that is to say, where we are as a culture, the developmental issues that are unique to women, a topic very popular in the 1980s, as well as how clergy can effectively address their audiences in the language of more than one stage so that their message fits the developmental diversity of their audience.

While development is an individual project and a personal responsibility, the quality of development in a society can be described by a distribution curve where there are outliers in the lower end as well as the higher end of the curve with most individuals clustered in the midrange section. Thus, we can make generalizations about how our society is maturing. We can also make a calculated guess about particular people or characters in a story.

We can postulate with a good degree of certainty that adults who marry and take responsibility for their young children are in Stage 3 where bonding as a family unit is their paramount value. This is when empathy and connection are enhanced.

We propose that individuals who are overusing alcohol or other recreational substances, and who are either not partnered or married with conflicts about role definition, are in Stage 2 which is an impulsive stage, and are not yet adults though they have adult bodies. They may be married but they do not live up to their role responsibilities and they frustrate their partners.

Negotiation does not help these marriages. The impulsiveness of Stage 2 individuals is based on feelings and living in the moment, not responsibility towards their significant others. These are not the feelings of empathy and caring. This is why we do not consider Stage 2 people adults.

Stage 3 is a feeling stage that has internalized traditional morality. Harmony is valued. These individuals listen and aim to be cooperative. It is not hard to be a wave in Stage 3. On the other hand, the agreeableness of Stage 3 becomes a problem later when the individual begins to define their own needs and realize they have overcommitted to the needs of others.

Stage 4 creates distance from traditional values and commitments. It is about critiquing cultural norms and defining oneself as an individual with primary authority for one's life. This stage dethrones traditional wisdom and marches to its own drummer. It is a thinking stage, and empathy is generally missing. When one or both partners in a couple get to this stage, conversations are intense and hard to resolve because there is insufficient ability to hear and empathize with the other point of view. This is often when couples come to therapy.

It takes time for breakthroughs in knowledge to filter down to the lives of individuals. We believe this shift in an emphasis on individualistic thinking in our culture began with Sir Isaac Newton who initiated an epoch of science that elevated a confident, deterministic worldview. It has taken more than 350 years to unfold the meaning of this first scientific revolution and its impact on the development of individuals and society to play out its benefits and costs.

It has finally been successfully challenged by the new revolution in the science of quantum physics that understands boldly that the electron in its orbital is unlocalizable, that consciousness is not a material based phenomenon, and at the most detailed level of subatomic particles, reality is not determined. This highlights the opportunity for our creativity. The other aspect of the quantum field is how all life is connected. It is a dynamic paradox that can inspire us to take profound responsibility for ourselves and the communities we create together.

All of this is meant to contextualize the individualism and confidence of Stage 4 people who are leaders in our culture, and who represent significant accomplishment in personal development, but do not embody the zenith of human possibility. Their individualistic development is the fulfillment of the old science of Newtonian physics that objectifies the world as material and defines humans as capable of mastering it. This perspective lacks humility and heart which is a Stage 4 limitation for society as well as for romantic relationships.

The Role of the Human Brain in Creating Our Experience

From the perspective of neuroscience, Dr. Iain McGilchrist's[3] 20-year research project offers evidence to support our view of the cultural impact of the Newtonian revolution in science, as well as our stage development analysis with his comprehensive understanding of left-right hemisphere functioning. He comes to the same conclusion that what is missing in our current culture, meaning the last hundreds of years, is the holistic balance of thinking and feeling that the right brain offers the left brain. His research and analysis concludes we need the active engagement of both hemispheres, but the left hemisphere should serve the right hemisphere's integrated perspective.

Iain McGilchrist starts by asking, why is the brain divided and why is it asymmetrical when the head itself is symmetrical. He invested 20 years putting the research and the history of civilization together to draw his conclusions. Dr. McGilchrist explains convincingly that this bifurcation of the brain is not an accident. The brain has been bifurcated and asymmetrical even before insects and worms and includes reptiles, birds and mammals going back 700 million years. Further, he notes the corpus callosum that connects the two hemispheres in humans is involved in inhibiting the connection of the two hemispheres more than facilitating the connection.

We are meant to have two different ways of looking at the world. This is Dr. McGilchrist's conclusion and it is affirmed by his professional peers. The difference in the hemispheres is their way of attending. How we attend to the world determines what we find. The hemispheres have different reasons for existing and give us different ways of addressing the world.

The left hemisphere isolates particular things out of a bigger picture. It quickly jumps to conclusions, makes decisions, prizes certainty. Its evolutionary origins are seen in the need for a bird to distinguish the seed that they can eat from a rock or grains of sand. The left hemisphere can pick out the things that are known that can be carried and picked up and used.

The right hemisphere, on the other hand, is focused on the unknown, on the predator. To avoid being eaten by a predator while an animal in the vicinity is hunting for food requires having an awareness that is interested in discovery and exploration. This hemisphere knows it needs to have more information. It knows that it doesn't know. This is so unlike the left hemisphere that needs certainty to know and has confidence in its knowing. It does not know what it doesn't know, and is not interested.

At this point, the descriptions of left and right hemisphere functioning should be reminiscent of our discussion of the distinctions of listening and responding as a wave or particle. Dr. McGilchrist proceeds to make a historical and cultural case for how our culture has changed from right brain dominant to left brain dominant in the last few hundred years. This is an affirmation of our thesis that the cultural impact and developmental accomplishment that is a consequence of Newton's revolution in science has put pressure on our romantic relationships to create love from the rational and particle-ized version of ourselves where we don't have the patience and empathy to be truly open-hearted when we reach the individuated Stage 4 level of competence. Dr. McGilchrist offers a direction for a solution that is complementary to our approach. We will come back to that later.

Dr. McGilchrist asks an important question: Why has it been important for evolution to preserve these two ways of knowing? His focus is his concern about the over-emphasis of the left brain in our western culture. His analysis of brain research and his exploration of our two-thousand-year civilization brings him to the conclusion that the left hemisphere is ideally suited to do the administrative work that grows out of the right hemisphere's holistic perception of reality.

He calls the right hemisphere, "the master," and the left hemisphere, "the emissary," highlighting his conclusion that an administrative role for the left brain that serves the right hemisphere's vision is in the best interests of our individual life as well as our culture.

He laments the developments in the last few hundred years in western civilization that has let the left brain dominate and how this has had an enormous impact on how we pay attention to everything in our world. This points to the quality of how we relate to everything and everyone. It is hard to sustain the energy of a romantic relationship if our left brains are reducing our partners to pragmatic functions and we are impatient and draw conclusions quickly.

Remarkably, Dr. McGilchrist points out that all forms of higher animals including birds, mammals, reptiles, and humans have split brains. The left brain in humans is focused and explicit; it maintains memories of facts and focuses on fixed and static information. It is rule governed and inflexible. It allows us to see the outside world as material to be manipulated. It focuses on the known.

The right brain focuses on the unknown and the evolving and interconnected nature of the world. As we have described in higher animals, this hemisphere provides vigilance in looking for predators in an unknown environment. This aspect of the right hemisphere serves humans in their openness; they are able to respond to unexpected dangers. Its appreciation of the unknown gives them an attentiveness that is "present." The right hemisphere in humans also allows for diffuse and unconscious processes. Thus, the right hemisphere is capable of an embodied empathy and personal narrative. It is open and can tolerate ambiguity and paradox.

Research has found that, in most cases, the left side of our brain usually functions in a focused, logical or rational way for speaking and solving problems. The left side of our brain deals with the known in our world. Everything shows up to the left brain as a localized, analyzable, focal, knowable, particle-like, objective-like, piece of information. The left hemisphere is better attuned to tools and to whatever is inanimate, mechanical and machine-like. Think about how much you use your left brain versus your right brain in your relationship interactions.

The right side of our brain functions in a non-linear way, for example, by enjoying music and appreciating paintings. The right side of the brain is responsible for perceiving the subtleties of a person's mood, facial expressions, and subtle hints behind spoken words. It is open to assessing an unknown situation and uniquely adapted to dealing with living things that are flexible, organic, and constantly changing over time as all living things are. The right brain is also responsible for creative inspiration of all kinds.

Applying this to the dynamics of relationships, when our right brain predominates, we experience the world and our partner in a calm way where we are comfortable with mystery. Romantic relationships can flourish in the mystery of romantic love. When the left brain predominates, we tend to think we know the way things should be and this produces a particle-like interaction in our romantic relationship.

Stroke patients offer a window into how couples function and malfunction. We can see the different functions of the right and left brains by studying people who experience strokes that damage one side of the brain. When the right side of the brain is damaged, the individual must rely on the left side of the brain to function. We find these right-brain injured people lose the ability to distinguish the individual. They only see categories like dogs or cats. For example, a farmer who loved his cattle and knew them all by name, loses the ability to distinguish them and only sees them as animals.

Right-sided stroke patients lose the ability to draw complex pictures. They can only draw stick-like figures. Right-sided stroke patients lose the ability to appreciate the implied meaning and feeling in speech and facial expressions, but they usually retain the ability to speak and write simple sentences. The faculties these individuals have lost in their right brain involve understanding the embodied nature of experience, the nuances of conversation. These functions highlight the holistic values that the right hemisphere contributes in its unique attention to life. If we allow the right brain to predominate, relationships can flourish in the mystery of romantic love. When the left brain predominates in our consciousness, we have a great need for certainty and this diminishes romantic passion.

These descriptions of stroke patients may be an extreme version of how you and your partner interact. Right brain stroke patients will lose their ability to perceive the left side of their body and the left side of the visual field. This is because the intact left brain controls the right side of the body and the right visual field. The right brain, when it is intact, is much more involved with both sides of the body rather than just focusing on the opposite side. Regularly, a right-brain stroke patient will deny that their paralyzed left hand belongs to them. They will deny that things exist on the left visual field. If you ask them what is on the street in front of them, they will report only things on the right side. If you walk them down the street and turn them around and ask them what is on the same street from the opposite direction, they will report only the things now on their right side of the visual field.

When you confront the stroke patient with the fact that they, just a few minutes before, reported all the things on the other side, they will get angry and irritable and deny the feedback. We can all see ourselves in this phenomenon. We get fixed in our limited point of view when we view our world from the contracted perspective as a particle and get irritable, defensive, and angry when others try to point out our view is limited. Seeing the world exclusively from the limited particle-creating left brain is problematic for relationships.

Now let us compare this with what happens to a left-brain stroke patient who is now using the right brain exclusively. The patient will still be able to perceive their whole body. They will still be able to draw pictures. Their perception of the world is intact but their ability to use it is impaired. They will often lose the ability to speak, read, write, work with numbers, logic and reasoning. Clearly, we need both our right and left brains to function well. However, the best balance in our lives is to have the holistic, right brain be the leader. This is Dr. McGilchrist's thesis.

When an individual allows the right side of the brain to predominate, this provides calm and movement as a wave. When the left side of the brain predominates with its value of rules and certainty, we are focused on the material and we become a particle and so does our view of the world. By appreciating and allowing the right brain to lead in our romantic relationship, we experience the joy of our wave nature. The left brain remains an asset for solving problems such as making a plan and accomplishing the details of the plan.

If you can see from Dr. McGilchrist's left/right brain stroke research, the mechanics of how the dominance of each side of the brain affects behavior, you will discover a new sense of compassion for yourself and your partner. The struggles of stroke patients may mirror what you and your partner are going through as you go from one stage to the next. You deserve the same kind of compassion that we give stroke patients. The good news is that you and your partner have the capacity to develop the skills that are missing as a result of your stage emphasis in thinking or feeling.

With longevity, each gender has the opportunity to emphasize bonding with each other and their children and also focus on competency skills for work. There is time for each partner to develop themselves as individuals and discover and practice their wave nature. It becomes the responsibility of each individual and each couple to appreciate the value of learning how to share and listen deeply to each other and respond to new emotional and practical needs that come from their evolution over time. This is the vision of relationship from the right hemisphere's point of view: a rich partnership of mutual development that includes bonding with friends and family, exploration and adventure, contribution to society, and a passion and gratitude for life.

Both partners in a relationship would be wise to practice and learn over time to allow the right brain to do what only it is capable of doing, which is to accept the mystery that your partner is to you and suspend judgments about each other. This leads you to an openness where you create your future through conversations that emanate from your wave nature. This is where the right brain is best at envisioning the possibilities of the future and sharing the vision in heart-centered conversation.

Accepting that our partner sees the world differently can help us maintain our wave-like nature. Trying to convince our partner to see the world the way we do will push us into left brain dominance and our particle-like nature. This will diminish the energy of love and appreciation we have for our partner.

Developing the left and right hemispheres of the brain and integrating their function in the service of the right brain's big picture of life is another way of describing the path to fulfilling the potential of a human life. This honors and balances the heart and the mind. Understanding the limitations of the left hemisphere's administrative and practical capabilities should sober us into seeking a harmonious relationship between the hemispheres. Too many of us in our personal and public lives rest prematurely with the satisfaction of functional competence in the workspace or an ideological framework that puts everything in order. This is not sufficient development for ageless love.

Eventually, as the meaning of the second revolution in science in quantum physics is digested in our culture, there will be a full appreciation for how the right brain is best suited to be the master with the left brain at its service. This will elevate the goal of integrating our heart-mind development to a higher value and priority. Our culture will then enhance its support of relationships and appreciate wisdom. Until then, we each need to be leaders in our own lives in taking responsibility for charting our own path for this development.

We understand that the full unfoldment of human development takes a lifetime of experience to integrate feeling and thinking at the level that fulfills the full potential of love in a romantic relationship. This is why we focus on skills. We can encourage and practice using our hearts and minds together in ways that approximate the full realization of our development before we get there. This deepens our experience of the journey of our human life.

The message of Dr. McGilchrist's work relates profoundly to the challenge of all relationships in our time. There is a general breakdown of communion in our society where it has become hard to tolerate differences of all kinds. The divorce rates and decreasing marriage rate reflects this same disconnection. According to Dr. McGilchrist, our left brain has become dominant and characteristically uses language, not for empathy or presence, but for a functional manipulation of the world. This message from Dr. McGilchrist matches our stage development assessment that the dominance of Stage 4 individualistic values overemphasizes administrative thinking at the cost of true caring and listening in our current culture.

The solution to this disconnection is to learn to listen and share with your partner as a valued, precious other. Dr. McGilchrist weaves a supporting theme into our analysis of stage development and highlights the challenge of enhancing and integrating the growth of heart and mind over a lifetime. The right brain is uniquely capable of seeing the big picture, creating presence, and appreciating uniqueness. Your differences with your partner are many and inevitable. One of the goals of this book, and all of our courses, is to start the process of teaching you the skills to maintain your wave nature in your romantic partnership so you can grow and develop ageless love.

QUESTIONS TO PONDER:

- *Do you see yourself as allowing your right brain to be the master of your worldview, or is your left brain in charge of your world perceptions?*
- *Do you approach your partner or the people close to you with your practical, localizing left brain or your open-hearted right brain?*
- *What examples come to mind?*

CHAPTER 7

Living as a Wave

We have established that most individuals want loving relationships and this desire may be as deep as the foundational electrons in creation. How to keep love vibrant and growing has been our focus. We also explored a pattern of electron bonding that grows in complexity over time as atoms grow in complexity. This mirrors human development. We explored how individuals develop over a lifetime, and how this evolution of our experience of our "self" impacts our partnership. Sometime in our 30s or 40s when we are knee deep in our marriage and family relationships, we are likely to become more individuated and invested in our thinking function. This is good for work and good for problem-solving practical complexities. However, it poses a challenge for romantic relationships.

Neuroscience offers the same message from a different perspective. It says that as a culture, we have overinvested in our left brain. The left brain reinforces our particle nature and an administrative pragmatism that is closed to feelings and the bigger picture of life. This highlights the dilemma of romantic relationships: at the same time, we are committed to profound love, we do not have the resources to deliver on our promise.

It is not possible to accelerate the holistic development of individuals beyond their life experience. It takes a lifetime to refine the personality and develop wisdom that cultivates the heart. However, we can introduce and practice skills that create and enhance connection. We can teach you how to be a wave by intention. Skills give us the tools to listen, share, and discover what we want and need from each other while we grow into the wisdom of life. We invite you to learn and practice living your relationship life as a wave.

Prescriptions for the Mind
LIVING AS A WAVE IN YOUR ROMANTIC RELATIONSHIP

Rx #1: Understand life stages

Understand and accept that in a long-term romantic partnership, you will not always experience a smooth ride over the years.

The prescription is to understand life stages:

- *People grow through life and move from feeling close to those they love to feeling more separate and autonomous from those they love. We have outlined the inevitable changes that occur over an adult's lifetime.*

- *The transitions are usually not smooth and comfortable for either partner. Delay big decisions about your relationship when you or your partner are going through a stage transition.*

- *By accepting your partner's changes, you can become the best lover with this perspective. When you can understand and accept your own and your partner's development, there will no longer be a need to hide your feelings. You will be able to listen to your partner with a much bigger perspective about what they are going through. You can care about your partner's world, their pain and struggles, their worries, fears and desires when you do not personalize it to mean something negative about you.*

- *To enhance your understanding about the spiral of personal development read our book* The Marriage Map: The Road to Transforming Your Marriage from Ordeal to Adventure.
- *Commit to learning new skills to navigate through these changes.*

Rx #2: Make appointments for conversations

- *When you have a serious or sensitive subject to discuss, make an appointment with each other so that you both can give the conversation your undivided attention.*
- *Couples are surprised how much more effective and caring their discussions can become with just this step.*

Rx #3: Listening without interrupting

- *Practice focused listening, which means listening without interrupting.*
- *Try asking your partner, "Would you like for me to just listen to you so I can really understand what you're feeling and how you see things?"*
- *Notice how long you can listen without planning your response or interjecting your point of view. We recommend 3 to 5 minutes.*

Rx #4: "It would really make me happy if . . ."

In a positive way, share the specific behaviors that describe how you want to be treated by your partner. Say, "It would really make me happy if . . ."

- *Appreciate your partner when they attempt to accommodate your requests, even when their effort falls short of your expectations.*
- *It takes time to learn about each other's sensitivities. When you gently give clear feedback and say, "Ouch," and then ask for the behavior that you want, this allows your partner to correct their behavior without a negative emotional consequence.*
- *Many of these recommendations may seem simple but often take practice to feel natural and heartfelt, especially after couples have*

fixed patterns of communicating. The workshops we teach give couples a chance to practice and share their questions and concerns in a warm, authentic environment.

Rx #5: Understanding your differences

Explore the idea that you and your partner are different in how you see the world. Accepting your differences creates a more authentically happy relationship.

- *Hearing your partner's perspective and interpretations, and understanding their perceptions will be different from yours, you will learn to not judge them, and your partner will learn to not judge you.*
- *This leads to understanding each other and clarity about what you want from each other.*

Rx #6: Distribute chores and responsibilities

- *Distribute distinct chores and responsibilities for each partner so that you can appreciate your partner for what they do.*
- *Men love to do things for their partner, and they love the praise that they get for doing it. This creates the energy and enthusiasm for romance.*
- *Splitting up tasks 50-50 promotes being roommates and business partners. We suggest each partner has their own areas of responsibility.*
- *Maintaining novelty, sensuality and the joy of the man and woman differences requires enhancing and embracing male-female qualities.*

Rx #7: Imagining your ideal relationship

In the quantum field, there are unlimited possibilities. Therefore, we want you to think about what you want for yourself in your romantic relationship.

- *Be specific. Imagine and visualize scenes of your heart's desire for love, respect, and weaving your lives together in a creative expression of your unique personalities.*
- *The more real you make the scenes and feelings that arise from your desire, the more you tap into the quantum field.*

Rx #8: Learning skills for ageless love

To experience what you most desire—a great love and ongoing expansion of the heart and mind with a partner—take concrete steps.

- *Identify the barriers that are holding you back from the ageless love you want to create.*
- *Then, learn the skills for navigating these challenges so you can experience a deeper connection.*

The real secret to ageless love is for you and your partner to open yourselves to an inner expansion of your minds and hearts. Then together, you can overcome all of your challenges.

But first, you have to understand the barrier responsible for your conflicts. Then you can discover the skills needed to confront that barrier. As a reader of this book, we want to invite you to a quiz that will make it easier for you . . .

Our free online quiz will help you identify what issues are having the most significant impact on you and your partner. You can take it here: agelesslovebook.com/resources

Then once you've completed the quiz you will know exactly what's holding you back. You will also discover a solution that enables you to work on your barriers with our support and guidance. With this help, plus what you have learned in this book, you will be well on your way to creating ageless love.

SECTION #2

THE BODY:
The Physiology of Ageless Love

by Michael J. Grossman, M.D.

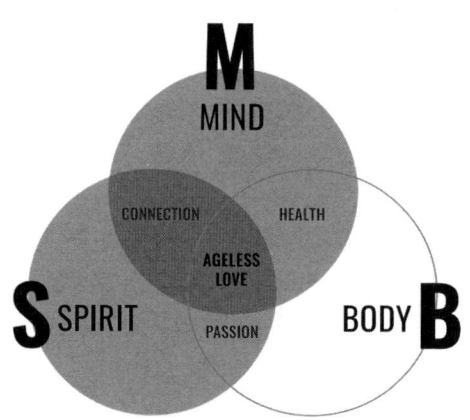

Introduction

In our introductions to the book, Barbara and I each wrote about the momentous changes that are occurring in medicine and science. It takes change on such a large scale to accelerate progress and growth. Having been exposed and then immersed in the principles of meditation in my career as a doctor, I have kept an open mind to new ways of thinking that are consistent with those principles.

When I was in medical school in the 1970s, I was taught that illness and disease were predominantly controlled by your genes. Health and longevity were predetermined. When I told my professors in medical school that I thought that diabetes was caused by eating too much sugar, the response was laughter. "Everyone" knew that diabetes was a genetically determined disease and I was just a foolish medical student. Over time, science discovered that only a very small portion of diabetes, about one percent, is genetically determined. Was I ever proven to be ahead of the times!

I did research on meditation before and after I graduated medical school. I learned to be a teacher of meditation in 1973. I taught thousands of people to meditate. I became licensed in acupuncture in 1974, one of the first licensed acupuncturists in the United States when President Richard Nixon opened up our relationship with China. Acupuncture seemed to be a bizarre science that amazed my professors and fellow medical students back in those days.

Treating ill people in 1974 with acupuncture was an extraordinary breakthrough for medical science. It held secrets about the body that allowed the body to heal and respond in ways that had nothing to do with prescription drugs. For years after medical school, I combined herbs, nutrition, acupuncture, chiropractic, and other natural approaches to detoxify the body to allow the body's natural, inherent healing power to restore health and vitality.

In the 1980s, when I first heard about treatments to reverse yeast infections in the G.I. tract with herbs and prescription medicines, I laughed. "Everyone knew" that this was a harmless organism that could not really hurt anybody. Just like my medical school professors, this was so far out of the box of my thinking I could only laugh. While yeast is seemingly harmless, research showed it can irritate the gastrointestinal tract and create leaky gut syndrome.

Over time, I learned to appreciate the G.I. tract is the key to how our body responds to the environment around us. 75 percent of the immune system lymph tissue surrounding the gastrointestinal tract are the detectors of foreign invaders that tell us through testing what is going on in our body on a chemical and cellular level. I was an early practitioner of functional medicine advanced by Dr. Jeffrey Bland Ph.D. My first book *The Vitality Connection: 10 Practical Ways to Optimize Health and Reverse the Aging Process* was written in 2002. I enjoy being on the cutting edge of new developments in medical science.

In 2009 I joined the BodylogicMD group of physicians who specialize in bioidentical hormone replacement therapy to reverse the aging process. We can positively affect longevity by replacing bioidentical hormones that diminish as we age. The science of staying youthful has exploded.

The most recent epigenetic research clearly indicates that the environment signals which genes will be expressed, and which ones will be inactive. This depends upon our nutrition,[4] the chemistry of our environment, and the signaling factors expressed by our thoughts and emotions.

Topping off longevity research is the Harvard study started by George Valiant, M.D. and continuing over 80 years. This research is discussed here in the mind section, and clearly shows longevity after the age of 50 years old is significantly related to the quality of your intimate relationships. Wow! Does that upset traditional medical beliefs.

Understanding how to create ageless love will require looking at the mind, body and spirit in order to create the environment that signals to our DNA to express genes that create age reversal. In the mind section, we explored what it takes to create ongoing vibrant and passionate romantic love as it is an essential part of longevity.

The 1990s brought a dramatic new understanding of how genes work in our body. In medical school in the 1970s I was taught that our genetic code determines diseases and longevity. The official word back then was that you are stuck with whatever bad genes you have, and their expression is fixed.

Mendelian science from the Middle Ages said that genetic traits are dominant or recessive. You receive one set of genes from your mother and one from your father. That means you can have one recessive and one dominant gene or two recessive or two dominant genes. Purple flowers will produce purple offspring unless recessive traits happen to be combined, and then you might get a white flower. These were the options. The dominant gene from either parent will produce the dominant gene trait. If you get a recessive gene trait from both parents, then you get the recessive gene expressed.

Now comes the breakthrough of epigenetics which means "above genetics." In the 1990s a strain of agouti mice were carefully genetically bred to get diabetes, heart disease and cancer at an early age. They looked fat and yellow, unlike healthy mice who looked brown and thin. These genetically programmed, sickly mice allowed the researchers to study these common medical problems. The succeeding generations also became sickly at a very young age.

The whole understanding of inherited genetic traits was turned upside when a later generation of agouti mice were fed high doses of B vitamins and folic acid during pregnancy.[5] Their offspring were normal looking and had a normal lifespan.

Further, their children and grandchildren and all future offspring who were fed ordinary diets also looked normal and had normal life spans.

This should inspire you to live and eat healthily and use nutrients to redirect your genes to create your health and your children's health for all future generations.[6] In addition, we encourage you to follow the recommendations from doctors who use herbs and nutrients, and who restore natural hormone levels and utilize stem cells and growth factors as part of a full anti-aging regimen to reprogram your genetic code. You can create for yourself and your loved ones an expanded lifetime of good health and vitality by following our prescriptions at the end of each section of the book.

CHAPTER 8

The Chain-Link of Physical Vitality and Longevity

In the Mind section we described how essential the quality of our personal relationships is for longevity. Our emotions and our thoughts are critical to creating a healthy environment in our body for cells to express healthy longevity genes. Our cells are protein producing machines. All cells except red blood cells produce proteins which are essential to our health and well-being. Imbalances that come from negative emotions and negative thinking as well as environmental toxins and eating poorly can negatively affect our genetic expression.

As a result of our imbalanced thoughts and feelings, poor lifestyle choices and environmental toxicity, there are many imbalances that accumulate in our physiology. As these imbalances add up, and as unhealthy genes are expressed, we gradually develop habits and patterns that make us feel like we are heavy particles pushing through our daily activity. We lose our vitality and our youthful enthusiasm. It becomes harder and harder to be our best self.

In this Body section, we will look at restoring our wave nature on a physical level by mechanically dissolving the imbalances that have accumulated in our body and cause us to feel like a particle: tired, heavy, and feeling at the mercy of people and things around us.

As an anti-aging physician, one of the foundational things that I do is enhance vitality for men and women by replacing declining hormones as we age with bioidentical hormones that restore a balance to their physiology. I also use other natural technologies to repair the body. Romantic passion requires a healthy body that will support passion. In quantum mechanical terms, we want to feel like a wave where we are creative, non-localizable, and enthusiastically moving through our life. When we feel tired or constricted by stress, or unwell in any way, we are localized like a particle; we have lost the feeling of all possibilities and we restrict our movements.

It is hard to feel passionately in love when we are tired, overweight, or foggy brained or when we are caught up in our particle nature and feel angry, hurt, resentful or depressed. Our intellect can tell us that we feel love, but it is hard to deliver love when we feel trapped in an ill or tired body. When we feel healthy in our body, we have the energy and enthusiasm to actively engage in the activities that make romantic love blossom. In the following chapters, you will find a practical guide on how to apply the latest science of restoring health and vitality to your physical body.

I have integrated the use of natural human bioidentical hormones in my practice of medicine since the 1980s. Prior to that time, only synthetic hormones were commonly prescribed. Research shows that synthetic hormones shorten the human lifespan because many physical illnesses occur after prolonged use of these synthetic products. On the other hand, natural bioidentical hormones have been shown to extend our life span, along with less heart disease, less cancer, better brain functioning and better quality of life. (see Appendix #1)

As a physician, this is a rewarding area for me to help patients because it creates emotional, mental and physical enthusiasm for doing things that increase youthfulness: eating healthy, exercising, rebooting sexual activity and new hobbies. As you become more active and engaged with people, you also gain the benefits of longevity that good relationships in general and romantic relationships specifically provide.

By implementing the recommendations discussed in this book into your routine, you can attain optimum levels of health, happiness, and vitality. This section provides time-tested and proven information you need to know to slow the aging process and enjoy a vibrant life.

You can choose to live with vitality until you are a 100 years-old or feel old and sickly at 65. Anti-aging was science fiction 25 years ago. Now it is a reality.

Creating vitality in the body takes a different mindset than creating vitality in the arenas of spirit and mind. To develop your spirit and mind, it is important to use the gifts you were born with to their maximum. If you have a gift of math and science, you are wise to focus on your talent and not try to be an artist or psychologist. Rather, you expand the gifts that you are naturally born with.

However, in the area of creating health, vitality and longevity in your body, you need to work on whatever aspect of your health is weak. Imagine that your physical health and well-being is like a chain link. If the chain breaks in any part, then you die. If you are strong in all physical areas except you don't exercise, or perhaps you are strong in all areas except you don't eat healthy, the area you are ignoring is your vulnerability. You may be healthy in many ways, but if you have a heart attack or if you get Alzheimer's or degenerative immune disorders like arthritis or lupus, this breaks the chain-link of health and well-being.

In this discussion of supporting ageless love with a healthy body, I will make many recommendations and I encourage you to focus on doing the things that represent strengthening your weakest link. Let us look at the various links in the chain of physical health.

CHAPTER 9

Balancing Hormones as We Age

The most foundational part of reversing physical aging after the age of 45 is balancing hormones. For unknown reasons hormone levels go down in men and women consistently after the age of 35. Athletes do not perform very well in their 40s because their hormone levels have dropped considerably. Most people do not really notice the loss of hormones and vitality until after the age of 45.

Women and Hormone Loss

For women, it is very dramatic when they go into menopause, usually between the ages of 45 and 55. Some women can begin having hot flashes and sweats when they are premenopausal.

They don't sleep as well at nighttime. They get moody and irritable. They lose their sexual libido. They lose their enjoyment and mental enthusiasm for doing and accomplishing things. Too many physicians are still practicing 1970s medicine and telling their patients to go off hormones after a few years because it may do bad things to you.

Research shows this caution about hormones is not true if you are using natural bio-identical hormones and if you are using them in a way where it is metabolized properly. Estrogen and testosterone should not be given orally to get maximum benefits of the natural hormones. When you use them orally the medicines are absorbed through the G.I. tract. Then they go through the liver and are metabolized into compounds that may not be entirely healthy for you. Women have been making these hormones naturally since their teenage years and they travel directly from the ovaries into the bloodstream. By using bio-identical hormones topically, the hormones go directly into the bloodstream as if they were produced naturally. Topically means using cream or patches or insertion of pellets under the skin.

Progesterone, specifically when taken orally, is metabolized into compounds that are very helpful to promote sleep and calmness, but it also can be used topically. These topical hormones can be obtained with prescriptions. Natural estrogen patches and progesterone capsules can be obtained at local pharmacies with a doctor's prescription. Testosterone for women, however, is not available except by compounding pharmacies as it is still not available from big pharmaceutical companies.

For women, estrogen is very important for brain functioning, memory, hot flashes and bone strength. You only need tiny doses. You don't need to re-start your menstrual cycle again in order to get the benefits. The progesterone you take can be a moderate dose which is very helpful for sleep and mood. Together with natural bio-identical estrogen, natural bio-identical progesterone can be very helpful to prevent cancer and heart disease. (See Appendix #1)

Testosterone is a more controversial area in prescribing to women. It is thought of by most physicians as a male hormone. However, women naturally have 1/10 of the testosterone that a man has throughout healthy adult life. Men, on the other hand, have 1/10 of the estrogen level and progesterone level of women. When women lose testosterone as they go through menopause, they will find that they cannot exercise the way they used to. They experience decreased muscle mass, extreme muscle fatigue and it takes their muscles a long time to recover. In addition, they lose brain clarity, general enthusiasm, and libido.

There are three ways for women to get testosterone. One is the cream that you apply daily which is a reasonable method and gives some benefits. The next method involves tiny needle injections, twice a week into the belly fat, which are relatively painless injections. This method offers more intense benefits than the cream.

Superior benefits are available with small, natural testosterone pellets, the size of a grain of rice, inserted under the skin into the fatty layer of the buttocks below the waistline. These are inserted about every three months. The benefits are greater because the testosterone that automatically releases from these pellets are in little spurts throughout the day, particularly with exercise. This is how the ovaries in young women naturally release testosterone. The intermittent spurts of testosterone released into the bloodstream seem to give the most benefits for restoring testosterone hormones to the physiology.

Besides these hormones, there are other hormones that can be very helpful for reversing the aging process. DHEA and Pregnenolone are naturally produced by the adrenal glands. They diminish significantly with aging. When these are taken orally you get increased mood, energy, and immune functioning, brain clarity, and reduced inflammation.

Bioidentical hormone replacement in post memopausl women is foundational to stop and reverse the aging process. After more than 20 years of prescribing bioidentical hormones I can say with certainty that it will increase youthfulness in your body, your mind and your emotions. Muscle stamina and strength and recovery increase. Brain clarity and enthusiasm for taking on life-affirming projects occurs. Libido and pleasure from sexual intimacy is a natural part of this process.

Men and Hormone Loss

Men do not experience a quick menopausal hormone loss like women. Rather, they go through andropause which is a very slow, gradual change in hormone levels. For men in their 50s, their hormones are definitely less than when they were in their 40s, and definitely less than when they were in their 30s. In general, men in their 50s notice very clearly that their energy level has diminished, their muscle recovery is slower, and their ability to build muscle is reduced. Also, brain clarity and enthusiasm are less. Men lose their male drive to accomplish and achieve and become more feminized as their estrogen levels go up.

This gets much worse at 60 years old and is incredibly less at 70 or above. Testosterone replacement in men can also be by cream, injections, or pellets. You have to be careful with cream as the woman in a man's life will easily get overdosed by touching his skin or clothes contaminated with the testosterone cream. I don't recommend it much for that reason.

Self-injections twice a week into the subcutaneous belly fat for men can be very helpful. We used to inject testosterone intramuscularly but it is quite a bit more painful. Many doctors still tell men to take injections every two weeks. The problem with a two-week interval is that you feel really good for four days and then really bad for 10 days. The testosterone does not last in the bloodstream more than four days. Over the last 12 years of practicing anti-aging medicine, I have men use testosterone injections twice a week in order to feel consistent benefits throughout the week.

The dose can vary and generally relates to the weight of the patient. The most effective method of giving testosterone to men is by pellets under the skin. Men will use 10 to 15 times as much as a woman. They usually can go approximately four months between pellet insertions. The benefits occur dramatically within a period of 10 days. Men consistently tell me, "This has changed my life."

Unfortunately, many doctors do not measure estrogen levels for men when they give them testosterone. As men get older, they move more testosterone back into estrogen, which can cause negative effects on their energy, their mood, and libido, and also cause increasing breast tissue. I usually use prescription medicine to lower their estrogen levels when I have them on testosterone replacement.

Men also will benefit from DHEA and Pregnenolone like women, but at much higher doses.

Almost all men over 60 years old will notice a dramatic change in their enthusiasm for accomplishment and their general energy and muscle stamina and endurance. Certainly they will notice increased libido. Bioidentical hormone replacement is an essential part in creating ageless love. (See Appendix #1)

Growth Hormone for Men and Women

Next, let's look at growth hormone which is so important for men and women as aging occurs. Growth hormone levels consistently and gradually get less and less as we age past 30 years old. The decline is a gradual process that affects all kinds of aging. Growth hormone is produced by the pituitary gland mostly as we sleep at nighttime. For some reason, while the pituitary gland has the ability to produce growth hormone, the signal to release growth hormone from the pituitary gland seems to disappear as we age. It is much cheaper and safer to use the signaling molecules to release your own growth hormone.

This loss of growth hormone affects the quality of our sleep and our dreaming which affects brain rejuvenation. It affects our ability to recover from exercise and build muscle. Loss of growth hormone increases body fat as we lose muscle. It affects our skin and increases wrinkling. I used to prescribe growth hormone injections to patients until about 2003, when laws were passed by Congress and enforced by the FDA which disallowed the use of growth hormone for anti-aging purposes. They did this because baseball players were hitting too many home runs. Isn't that interesting!

About 2015, we began using releasing factor peptides. These peptides are amino acid chains that are naturally in the body. Sermorelin is currently the one I like best, but others are available. Their function is to signal the release of growth hormone. These signaling factors can be injected into the belly fat with an insulin needle at bedtime five days a week and it is very, very effective to release growth hormone in any aging man or woman. The results are consistently efficacious. However, unlike testosterone, it takes two to four months to gain benefits.

The first benefits gained are better sleep and more dreaming. Then after two or three months, you begin to notice more muscle strength, stamina, endurance, muscle recovery, and more energy. Growth hormone acts as a conductor of the orchestra with the orchestra being all the other hormones required to stay youthful. Growth hormone was named because teenagers have a lot of it as they are growing very quickly. However, even after bones stop growing, growth hormone is needed to maintain the repair and upkeep of your physiology.

Test Hormone Levels

Some hormone levels can be tested easily by blood tests. However, some may need urine or saliva tests which measure hormone levels over 24 hours rather than the blood test which just measures one point in time. I like to keep my patients' levels in the youthful range of a 40-year-old. If your doctor says you have normal levels for your age of 60 or 70 years-old, beware. You want to feel like you are 40, not like 70.

CHAPTER 10

Treating General Fatigue

There are many causes for general fatigue. The most common cause, referred to earlier, is the general buildup of stress which occurs in modern life. Whenever we have a stressful experience, we get an increase in cortisol and adrenaline and other stress hormones. When the stress doesn't go away in a few minutes and continues day after day, we get very high levels of cortisol in our blood throughout the day. Over time of ongoing stress, the body begins to shut off the cortisol and adrenaline production and we get very low levels consistently throughout the day.

These low levels are associated with extreme fatigue, irritability and lack of enthusiasm. While caffeine can give you a quick boost temporarily, you then crash when it wears off and this ends up causing more adrenal fatigue. I treat many patients with this issue with a variety of natural herbs which can be very effective. These herbs are widely available; however, the quality is variable. I prefer to use certain vitamin companies which are very particular about how they process and purchase their herbal ingredients.[7]

These ingredients include rhodiola, ashwagandha, licorice, ginseng, and many others. When the fatigue has been going on for a long time and the adrenal glands are extremely burnt out, I will prescribe the actual hormone, hydrocortisone, to be taken several times a day. I prescribe these for just a short period of time until the herbal supplements can take over.

There are many other causes for chronic fatigue: food allergies, hypoglycemia, iron deficiency, and many other imbalances. This needs the attention of a health practitioner to play detective and sort out your particular circumstances.

One cause for chronic fatigue that is not related to aging can be low thyroid. Thyroid blood tests are very accurate and should include TSH as well as free T3 and free T4. If you fall out of the normal range you will probably need to take some thyroid supplementation regularly. Sometimes thyroid imbalances can relate to autoimmune problems called thyroiditis which can be detected with thyroid antibody tests. Treatment can vary but usually requires thyroid supplementation.

CHAPTER 11

Testing and Treating Early Artery Clogging

Clogging of the arteries is probably the number one cause of shortening your lifespan from a mechanical point of view. We have talked about how the quality of your relationship is the most important factor in longevity. However, when you don't feel the love, compassion, and joy of intimate personal relationships this has a big effect on your physiology and can create clogging of the arteries. The buildup of stress in the physiology will cause high blood pressure, arterial inflammation.

We used to think the clogging arteries came from "high cholesterol." However, there are a large percentage of people who have very high cholesterol and do not have clogged arteries. In addition, there are many people with low cholesterol who have clogged arteries. We now know that inflammation of the arteries is probably more important than the total cholesterol. Inflammation of the arteries can come from many causes. Some of them are mechanical but some of them are related to the buildup of stress in our physiology.

While you need to focus on the quality of your relationships for long-term health, longevity and vitality, you also have to start from where you are right now. You need to know how your arteries are doing. Early detection is a great technology which can allow you to avoid surgical interventions later such as coronary artery bypass and stent implants.

My favorite early detection test is an arterial stiffness evaluation. This involves either putting a sensor on your finger or a blood pressure cuff on your bicep. We can then use computers to measure the stiffness in your arteries. Before this clogging of the arteries takes place, the arteries get stiffer and that occurs five or 10 years before there is any clogging. We have natural, nutritional approaches which can stop this hardening and clogging process.

I like using nitric oxide supports,[8] and supports for the endothelial glycocalyx,[9] a microscopically thin gel layer that coats the vascular endothelium. I also use aged garlic which has been well researched[10] and shows that it will prevent and reverse atherosclerosis (arterial clogging).

The next level up for assessing arterial clogging would be ultrasound testing that includes intimal thickness. The first sign of the artery clogging is a thickening in the inner lining of the artery (intimal thickness) and then later it shows clogging. We can detect this on the ultrasound testing of the carotid arteries very easily which is a standardized test.

The next level of testing would be an ultrafast CT scan of the coronary arteries of the heart. This shows the calcium buildup within the arterial walls that closely corresponds to the clogging process. I do not suggest that you do these more than once every five years as there is a fair amount of x-ray exposure, but it is an excellent test to evaluate the level of artery clogging of the coronary arteries.

Another measure of early material clogging in the lower extremities is an ankle-brachial index. This measures the blood pressure in the arms and compares it to the blood pressure in the legs. If the legs have a lower blood pressure, it suggests there's clogging occurring in the arteries of the legs.

The usual testing of stress tests with echocardiograms are helpful but they only show clogging after it is there to a very significant extent. I prefer to catch it earlier and reverse it.

CHAPTER 12

Treat Prediabetes and Prevent Aging

A very significant cause of aging is the buildup of prediabetes. As blood sugar levels rise from being overweight and eating too much sugar and refined carbohydrates, we suffer from a buildup of advanced glycation end products. Most people in developed countries are much more overweight than they were 100 years ago. Abundant food and work that doesn't require physical activity is common. Unless you specifically work at regular exercise, becoming overweight is common and gradually leads to prediabetes and then full diabetes.

This buildup of the advanced glycation end products causes the proteins in the body to get stiffer and clogs arteries, causes skin sagging, affects vision, damages the kidneys, and affects the brain and adds to dementia problems. The good news is this is all preventable and it is easy to detect early before it becomes a problem and reverse it.

Testing should include hemoglobin A1c which is an average measurement of the blood sugar over the previous two months. This is much more accurate than just a fasting blood sugar measurement which can go up and down very rapidly in a short period of time. Hemoglobin A1c below 5.7 is considered normal but ideal would be

5.4 or less. Above 6.0 is considered the beginning of diabetes. 57 to 59 is getting to the not so good range.

We can also measure fasting insulin levels. Levels below 5 are excellent levels, above 20 is the beginning of diabetes. Insulin levels between 5 and 20 are considered pre-diabetic. If these tests are outside of the good range, we need to focus treatment on getting things back to a good range. Diet and exercise are critical. There are many good books written on this.

There are many herbs and nutrients that are very helpful to treat prediabetes. These include chromium, lipoic acid, cinnamon bark, vanadyl sulfate, gymnema leaf, and many others.[11]

CHAPTER 13

Inflammation and Longevity

The understanding of how inflammation is critical to health and longevity is still outside of the mindset of most physicians today even though the research is very clear. Inflammation is a major cause of aging and sickness. Inflammation is a major cause of artery clogging, brain dysfunction, muscle fatigue, and overall general fatigue. Over 70 percent of the immune system surrounds the gastrointestinal tract. Inflammation is generally related to processes that upset the immune lymphatics that surround the mouth, the throat, and the intestinal tract.

Having gas, bloating, diarrhea and/or constipation is not just an annoying thing. It is a very serious health problem. There are many causes for this inflammation. Some can relate to emotions and stress. Other causes are related to autoimmune problems such as allergies to foods and chronic yeast infections. Some relate to chronic gum inflammation. The treatment of these kinds of problems requires a physician who is interested and motivated to treat the whole patient and puzzle out the meaning of the presenting symptoms.

An easy way to test for inflammation is a test called ultrasensitive C-reactive protein which is a simple blood test that looks at the inflammation in the body. However, it is nonspecific. The test does not tell you if your inflammation comes from acute infection or some other chronic imbalance.

You will need to see a physician who practices what is called, "functional medicine." This type of medicine looks at the body as a complex network of interactions that needs to be methodically looked at, teased apart and then rebalanced. I often will put patients on a detoxification, food elimination diet which requires the patient to eat very simple foods like chicken, rice and vegetables along with a detoxification powder to assist in the clearing out of toxins. If a person feels dramatically better after 10 days of doing this, then the real work begins to find out which of the different foods need to be eliminated from their diet.

Sometimes treatment requires eliminating yeast and parasites. Sometimes it requires digestive enzymes of various sorts to assist in the digestion process. Sometimes it requires various probiotic bacteria to replenish a healthy bacterial flora.

shaken up." The body will respond immediately by sending stem cells and repair cells to the part of the body that has been vibrated and over a period of six weeks will repair any kind of damage that is occurring.

What is remarkable about this process is that we do not need to know specifically about the injury. We use the natural intelligence in the body to repair any kind of damage. The process usually involves six weekly treatments that each take about an hour.

We wait another six weeks to allow the repair process to occur and then evaluate the benefits. Research shows that 80 percent of the men who get this treatment are very happy with the results. I have found that men who have had problems for 10 or more years have created such disrepair that it may take more time to repair and may require more than six treatments.

The other process that I recommend for erectile dysfunction in men is platelet-rich plasma injected directly into the penis. These are tiny injections that are like little pinpricks from a blood test. The platelets are the little vesicles in the blood that create a clot when the body has been injured. The platelets then release growth factors which signal to the body, "Please repair this injured area! We are just holding it together with a clot" (fibrin matrix). The intelligence of the body figures out what needs to be repaired, whether it is an artery, or it is collagen, or it is nerves or muscles.

The platelet-rich plasma injections are natural and eighty percent effective in repairing erectile dysfunction. It also takes about six weeks after a single injection to evaluate the improvement. It may take two or three injections to get maximum improvement.

Another issue that men can have is called Peyronie's disease which is an injury to the erection mechanism. It occurs when the penis is actually bent out of shape when it is partially erect, and this cracks the little erection tubules. Over time you get scarring in the tubules and then the penis will curve in one direction or another depending upon where the damage has occurred in the penis. This usually affects the erection mechanism creating a diminished blood flow as the scarring gets heavier and heavier and closes off the tubules in different parts of the penis. Previously, and not so long ago, the only approach available for this problem was an enzyme treatment which was not very effective. The acoustic wave treatments and the platelet-rich plasma treatments are extremely effective in reversing Peyronie's disease. Sometimes it takes one treatment, other times multiple treatments, to return to normal curvature and erection functioning.

Other options for treating male sexual dysfunction include using one's own growth factors and stem cells. We will discuss later these newer, more intensive, repair stimulating factors that are available to repair any part of the body but are extremely effective in male sexual dysfunction. They are injected in the same way that the platelet-rich plasma is injected directly into the penis.

Femal Sexual Dysfunction

Female sexual dysfunction can also result from injury and damage to the vaginal area and the clitoris. This can include symptoms of painful intercourse which occurs from thinning of the vaginal mucosa and mechanical trauma related to childbirth. This can also occur from the aging process. Loss of the ability to experience pleasurable orgasms can occur from damage to internal nerves in the superior aspect of glands and nerves in the vaginal area as well as in the clitoris. This creates a lack of sensitivity and loss of the ability to have orgasm.

We can use the same technology that we use in men to restore sexual functioning in women. Platelet-rich plasma can be injected almost painlessly after numbing the area. Other options include Gainswave vibrational treatment, stem cells, exosomes, and other growth factors.

The same treatments that work for female sexual function will also work for loss of urine when coughing, sneezing, and exercising.

CHAPTER 15

Stem Cells and Exosomes for Age Reversal and Repairing Injuries

As we age, we gradually get wear-and-tear in our physiology causing our joints and collagen to thin out and then often tear. Pain in our knees and hips is very common as we grow older and develop wear-and-tear issues. We generally call this osteoarthritis. This degeneration can often lead to knee and hip replacement surgery. Pain can occur in any joint from the same problem. This can include symptoms in the shoulder, elbows, neck and back, etc.

Taking over-the-counter medication like Advil, Aleve, and Motrin or prescription anti-inflammatory medication can temporarily reduce the pain but have very negative long-term consequences. Side effects from these products include increased kidney problems, heart disease, and stomach ulcers. There are a lot of natural supplements that can be helpful. These include various collagen products, glucosamine, hyaluronic acid, as well as fish oil and SPM (specific Pro mediators), and fish oil concentrates.

However, the most effective and dramatic way to regenerate worn out, or torn or degenerated collagen in joints, tendons and ligaments is with focal injections of growth factors. The issue with collagen regeneration is that there is very little blood supply and very little signaling from the collagen to bring in growth factors to repair the damage. We can bypass this problem by injecting the growth factors directly into the injured area.

We can use the same type of growth factors that we would use in repairing male and female sexual dysfunction, starting with the very easy and completely safe use of platelet-rich plasma. This procedure uses your own blood and concentrates the growth factors in the blood. Then the growth factors are injected back into your body, either joint tendon or ligament. This takes less than an hour and will give you six weeks of ongoing repair. Then you have time to see if the problem is partially or totally repaired. You may need a second injection to get maximum improvement.

If the problem is more severe and your physician has suggested you will probably need a joint replacement, then you are a candidate for the more intensive repair process which can be done with injections of exosomes or stem cells. Stem cells are a more complex process which requires liposuction of your fat from your love handle or abdominal areas. One quarter cup of your fat is extracted and processed over several hours. Then the stem cells are injected directly into the injured part of your body.

We usually have enough stem cells to inject some of them intravenously. Intravenous injection allows the cells to swim all over your body and go to whatever area in your body needs more repair. This could be your brain, your heart, your kidneys, your lungs. The repair process from stem cells that is from your own adipose tissue will continue over six months. The intensity of repair is therefore much greater than from platelet-rich plasma which only repairs over a period of six weeks. With both processes, once the repairs occur, it stays.

Another option is to inject exosomes into the injured area. Exosomes are obtained from the umbilical cord of newborn babies. In the past we threw out the umbilical cords. Now we save the growth factors that are concentrated in the umbilical cords. These growth factors work very much like the growth factors from your adipose tissue to create six months or more of repair. They have the advantage of being very easy to defrost and inject and cost somewhat less than the adipose fat stem cells. There is a minor risk of injecting tissues when they are not your own, but careful screening for infection or viruses minimizes the risk.

Skin Rejuvenation

Reversing skin aging is an important part of an anti-aging program. When we look at ourselves in the mirror, what we see affects our beliefs about ourselves. If we see an old-looking person looking back at us, it creates thoughts and feelings which can be detrimental to our well-being and longevity. Skin aging is not inevitable and can be reversed.

This is a fun area for me to work in because I see how these treatments uplift my patients. Looking younger creates emotional and mental enthusiasm for participating in activities that increase youthfulness like eating healthy, exercising, and romance. Maintaining romance requires giving attention to your appearance. As already mentioned, romance and sexual activity are very good for your longevity.

How to Reverse Skin Aging

We have a variety of technologies for reversing the skin aging process. There are many topical antioxidants which are very important to maintain youthful skin that glows and is free of wrinkles. This includes vitamin C, vitamin E, Retin A (a derivative of vitamin A), ferulic acid, an antioxidant found in plants, resveratrol antioxidant and many others.

Various peptides can also be used topically to signal repair of skin. Peptides are various signaling proteins which occur naturally in the body and do a variety of things such as growing new collagen in the skin to repair it, making it look more youthful. Peptides can be combined with hyaluronic acid, a natural collagen needed by the skin to restore moisture and repair the skin collagen.

These various topical applications of antioxidants, peptides, etc. can over time improve the youthfulness of the skin very gradually. However, when skin has aged and not had the benefit of these kinds of products, and perhaps suffered from sun damage which promotes the aging process in the skin, then we can utilize more intense applications of anti-aging technologies.

My favorite technology is the pro fractional CO_2 laser which is a breakthrough in technology approximately around 2010. Prior to this, the CO_2 laser would remove your total outer layer of skin and take about a month or two to recover and might leave hypo pigmentation as a permanent complexity. This was definitely a consideration, but it did help dramatically to reduce sagging and wrinkled skin.

Now we have newer technology which results in only a few days of downtime. This technology uses a computer to create hundreds of little tiny pinholes in the skin with a CO_2 laser that will remove only about five percent of your total skin. Each little pinhole that is created stimulates the body to repair these holes and as it does, it improves the collagen elasticity and softness all over the skin. This produces a smoother, softer, tighter, less-wrinkled, more glowing skin. It is a dramatic procedure to make your skin look more youthful.

I recommend adding platelet-rich plasma or exosomes to your skin right after the treatment. This will immediately stop the discomfort and start a dramatic stimulation of healing and repair. Platelets are naturally in the skin and create a clot any time there is an injury. These release growth factors signal, "Please repair this area."

Exosomes are tiny little vesicles, smaller than a cell, that are derived from umbilical cord or amniotic fluid. They contain all kinds of growth factors that stimulate growth and repair. These products release growth factors that will allow your skin to heal like a 20-year-old which means less recovery time and more dramatic repair can occur. The benefits of the CO_2 laser last for many years.

There are many other procedures that can produce a more youthful look including a variety of injectable products that will add collagen to the face to reduce the effects of sagging. We used to think that aging faces were mostly related to sagging skin and loss of elasticity. While this is a factor, a bigger factor is the loss of volume in the skin which occurs because we lose fat in the face. Healthy, youthful fat under the skin allows us to have a youthful looking face. Older people have thinner skin because they have lost volume. It is like letting out the air in a balloon and the balloon sags, not because it lost elasticity, but because it has lost volume. Some of these volume products will last for 15 months, some will last for two years, and some for five years.

Bellafill will last for five years or more as it is a PLMA product that contains microscopic, little spheres of inert material to stimulate your own collagen to grow around it. Sculptra is a product of lactic acid crystals. Lactic acid is naturally produced when your muscles get overly used. Sculptra will stimulate collagen growth when injected under the skin and lasts for two years. The longest lasting hyaluronic collagen-type product, Voluma, can last for 18 months. There are many variations of the hyaluronic collagen-type products.

Another effective method of reducing skin aging utilizes microdermabrasion which creates tiny little pinholes in the skin and then we apply platelet-rich plasma or exosomes to the skin. The platelets or exosomes will release growth factors that call the stem cells to repair your skin, making it look more youthful. While this is not as intense a process as the CO_2 laser, it is much easier with very little downtime.

CHAPTER 16

Sleep Issues:
SLEEP APNEA

Sleep apnea is a very common problem as men and women get older. It occurs most commonly when there is a loss of elasticity in the throat tissues. The loss of elasticity causes a collapse of the airways while you are sleeping and you cannot get the air to go in and out. Disrupting the breathing cycle will cause you to lose oxygen in the blood and will partially awaken you from deep sleep to take in a deep breath. Heavy snoring may be a sign of sleep apnea.

This disruption of the sleep cycle can produce a variety of long-term health issues such as: excessive daytime sleepiness, morning headaches, irritability, limited attention span or difficulty thinking clearly, high blood pressure and heart disease.

It is a big health problem. It is diagnosed by having an overnight sleep study which measures your oxygen and your sleep disruptions. Treatment may include several kinds of approaches. Weight loss can be very helpful. Usually, the most common treatment is what we call a CPAP machine which creates positive airway pressure while you are sleeping through either nose prongs or a facemask. Other options include mouthpieces, and a new option is an electrical called Excite, used in the daytime to strengthen the b throat and tongue. I encourage you not to overlook this very serious health problem.

QUESTIONS TO PONDER:

- *What are your weakest links in the chain of health and longevity?*
- *Are there reasons why you may hesitate to address these?*
- *What would encourage you to address them?*

Prescriptions for the Body
MOVING TOWARDS AN "AGELESS BODY" AND FIXING THE WEAKEST LINK IN THE CHAIN OF HEALTH

Rx #1: Check hormone levels

"What You Should Ask Your Doctor?" Ask your doctor to check your hormone levels by blood, saliva, or urine levels.

- *Men should check after the age of 45 or younger if there are issues with muscle stamina or libido.*
- *Women should check after the age of 45 or younger if there are issues with hot flashes, sleep disturbance, moodiness, brain fog, loss of muscle stamina or decreased libido.*
- *Hormone imbalances in younger women commonly present as premenstrual moods.*
- Ask to replace hormones as naturally as possible.

For Men:

- *Testosterone may be given by daily cream or injections that you give yourself twice a week or tiny pellets under the skin every four months. Medications will be needed to reduce estrogen, i.e. anastrozole*

For Women:
- Replacement testosterone and estrogen and progesterone will probably be needed.
- Estrogen replacement may be creams or patches.
- Progesterone may be capsules or cream.
- Testosterone may be cream or pellets under the skin or subcutaneous injections.
- Only use natural human hormone replacement.

For Men and Women:
- Also check levels of DHEA, Pregnenolone, and growth hormone (IGF-1).

Rx #2: Test and treat artery hardening

Ask to Check Your Arteries for Early Hardening and Thickening.
- Arteries should be checked after the age of 45 or if you have a strong family history or if you have problems with cholesterol or diabetes.
- Check for the option to test for arterial stiffness. This is the earliest sign of an artery problem, much earlier than actual clogging.
- *Request CT scan X-ray for Calcium score of coronary arteries.*
- Request ultrasound of carotid arteries with intimal thickness score for early detection.

Rx #3: Reduce inflammation

Reduce Inflammation: The Cause of Heart Disease; Cancer; Arthritis; Autoimmune Disease.
- Ask for a screening test: C-reactive protein-highly sensitive. This blood test is a general measurement of inflammation which, if elevated, may require a variety of interventions.

- Balancing the GI tract is essential to reduce inflammation: getting to the cause of intestinal upsets, gas, bloating, constipation, and diarrhea.
- *Fish oil and other* anti-inflammatory herbs *may be needed.*
- *Looking for gum disease is very important.*

Rx #4: Check for prediabetes

Check for Prediabetes.
- Get a blood test for Hemoglobin A1C = average blood sugar over the past two months.
- 6.0 or more is diabetes, below 5.7 is okay but lower is better.
- Measure Insulin fasting: below 5 is good, 20 = diabetes.

Rx #5: Ideal blood pressure

Measure Blood Pressure.
- Below 130/80 is the best.

Rx #6: Reversing sexual dysfunction

Reverse Sexual Dysfunction.
- Consider acoustic wave therapy, (i.e., Gainswave).
- Consider p-shot or o-shot (with platelet-rich plasma, exosomes, or stem cells).

Rx #7: Natural treatments for non-healing injuries

Repair Joint Degeneration or Tendon and Ligament Non-Healing Injuries.
- Ask for a treatment with platelet-rich plasma, stem cells or exosomes.

Rx #8: Treating sleep apnea

Treat Sleep Apnea.
- *If you suffer from daytime sleepiness, irritability, brain fog, or snoring: seek testing for overnight sleep apnea screening.*

Rx #9: Motivation for anti-aging program

Find a Physician who will help to motivate you to start a comprehensive anti-aging program.
- See list of physicians in the Appendix or call my office for referrals.

SECTION #3

THE SPIRIT:
Connecting to the Field of All Possibilities

by Michael J. Grossman, M.D.

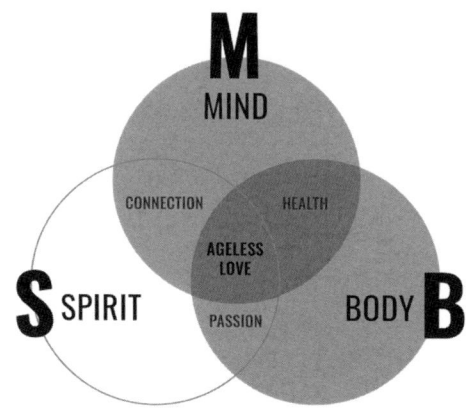

Introduction

My orientation as a scientist, a physician, and in my personal life was formed by early experiences that opened me to looking at the big picture of life. I learned early to look outside conventional thinking for solutions that are more effective, more natural, and support the harmonious and integrated health and development of the individual and their relationships.

Let me share an experience I had as a teen that expanded my world and opened me to the possibility of living my life as an adventure, with an open mind and heart, away from dread and worry. I would not have known to say at the time that this was a breakthrough in experiencing life as a wave, but in retrospect, it was certainly an invitation.

When I was 13, I had a brush with serious illness when I developed a reaction to a medication that created a two-year, severe hepatitis with jaundice and ongoing exhaustion. I changed from a happy-go-lucky kid to a serious thinker about life and death. As a 16-year-old college student, I became preoccupied with reading serious existential philosophers about the meaninglessness of life. I felt great existential despair and nausea while feeling that there was no meaning to life.

The breakthrough, quantum change in my perspective came while walking up a tree-lined hill to my NYU campus in the Bronx. I closed my eyes and prayed deeply, "If there is a God, please show me a way to see life differently." Immediately on opening my eyes, I caught a view of a peculiar maple tree that was right in front of me. It had metal growing out of its trunk. I couldn't understand how that could be. I circled the tree in bewilderment. The metal was generally in an up-and-down direction.

Wow! An instantaneous picture came into my mind. This tree had been a baby tree with a metal fence around it to hold it in place. As the tree grew its trunk, gradually the tree trunk expanded beyond the metal and almost entirely engulfed it.

The tree could have struggled, like a particle, to push the metal fence away because it felt like an obstruction. Instead, the tree behaved like a wave and accepted the metal fence and gently grew around it and integrated the metal fence into itself.

This, for me, is a living metaphor for how to overcome limitations in your life. Rather than obsess and complain about it or resist and resent it, by accepting what is happening as a part of your life without emotional resistance, you can grow in wisdom and beyond it.

My passion became, like the tree with the metal fence, to see the bigger picture of life. I found that by accepting life's limitations of sickness and death, I saved a lot of energy by not feeling sorry for myself. I didn't complain about my challenges, resist them, or resent them. Rather, my acceptance allowed me to grow beyond the limitation and become more effective in my life.

This approach, as I see it now, involves living in your wave nature and stepping into a possible future rather than obsessing about the limitations and difficulties in your path. The obsessing and stressing amounts to living in your particle nature which makes life more difficult.

Giving up complaints about perceived limitations, resentments, anger, hurts, injustice, guilt, and shame can allow us to be free of the past and open to creating possibilities in our future. We will discuss more about this metaphor later.

In college I was extremely stressed trying to get "A" grades in order to be accepted into medical school. The stress before exams made it almost impossible to sleep, and I suffered temporarily from headaches and nausea. Once the exam was over, I immediately felt relaxed even before knowing how I did on the exam. It struck me that this was no way to live life. I was inspired to learn meditation which totally changed my experience of taking exams. I felt a great relief of peace that filtered through all parts of my life.

With my experience of opening to the mysteries of life through the experience of the tree and metal fence, and the experiences that I encountered with deep meditation, I became a very open-minded kind of scientist. I was open to seeing the deeper connections beyond the mechanical Newtonian world of particle interactions. I was always pushing the envelope of medical science.

Spirit is Your Connection to Your Wave-Like Nature

In the section on the mind, we explained how the quality of your intimate relationships are critical to your physical well-being and longevity. We discussed how interacting from your wave-like nature is essential to sustaining the connection in your passionate romantic relationship. In the section on the body, we described the importance of paying attention to the weakest physical link in your chain of longevity links in order to enhance your health and vitality. Now we will explore the area of your spiritual connection and how it relates to longevity, quantum science and ageless love.

Let us look at the big picture of modern science to stretch our beliefs about what is possible in our lives and how we can grow into an unknown and incredible future free from our past limitations.

CHAPTER 17

Spirit:
YOUR SOURCE FOR A LOVING FUTURE

In the first two sections of the book, The Mind and The Body, we focused on the outer parts of ourselves. The outermost part is our body and our physical well-being. The mind and emotions are more inner than the body but there is a great relationship between the mind and body as they have a deep interconnection. There is still a more inner part of our self which goes beyond the mind that we can call our spirit, or our consciousness.

Consciousness and spirit are very related and intimate parts of our being. We can define consciousness as the most inner part of our being which is purely the witness part of ourselves. Our spirit is the part of ourselves that is deeply connected to our will and our deepest desires.

Consciousness is that part of ourselves which is silent but sources the energy that gives us life. This deep, unbounded, pure consciousness is filled with the energy of life. Whatever it is that leaves our body at the moment of death, weighs nothing, and yet dramatically moves us from vital living to a body that is no longer alive. What leaves our body according to many spiritual traditions as well as numerous reports from individuals who have had near-death experiences, is our consciousness and our spirit that moves to a different plane of existence.

The science of quantum physics helps us to understand how this can be. Quantum mechanics describes that the vacuum of outer space is not empty, but rather, filled with all possibilities. Subatomic particles are jumping in and out of the emptiness of space. Particles come and go in the field of emptiness and are vibrating and shimmering. Outer space is not empty but rather filled with energy and intelligence.

Our consciousness can connect us to this unbounded realm of infinite energy and intelligence while we are alive in our body. Meditation offers this experience. Our mind can experience the quantum field of pure consciousness, that is, consciousness without any thoughts. This is energizing and renewing and connects us to an awareness that we can create and grow our lives by giving our inspiration a direction. This is our pure wave nature. The experience of pure consciousness is called the field of all possibilities by meditators because it is a deep dive into our essential nature that we bring back to our activities.

When we describe this quantum state in the subatomic world, we say that the tiny subatomic particles are filled both with uncertainty and at the same time, all possibilities. When an electron is a wave, it has all possibilities. The electron cannot be localized in its orbital. It is somewhere in the vicinity, but it cannot be pinned down to a specific location. It can move without crossing space to get where it wants to go. It seems miraculous to scientists, and it was a head scratcher for science for a long time, but it is what happens.

However, when an electron becomes a particle and loses its wave nature, it becomes localized and knowable and loses its access to the realm of all possibilities. This is a metaphor for what happens in our lives. and what happens when we experience pure consciousness in meditation and then come out of the experience with thoughts.

When we experience stress, we are pushed out of the realm of all possibilities and we focus on the immediate danger that confronts us. In the Mind section we discussed the ongoing stress in our lives that stimulates our sympathetic nervous system. We also discussed how modern life encourages an overstimulation of this survival stress response, and specifically how our romantic partner relationship can be very stressful when we come up against our limitations in listening, sharing, and working out our different needs for love.

There is much more than just the stress response that is damaging to our lives and longevity. The stress response focuses us on outside stimuli. Earlier in the book, we wrote about the focus on objects, animals and other people who might be a danger to our immediate survival. When in danger, we focus on objects and time. How far is the tree for you to jump and climb to survive? How can we escape this torturous conversation where we feel criticized? We become focused on being a victim of our environment.

Contemporary life has created the intensity of busyness, and it is easy to miss the opportunity to be in touch with our deeper connection to the source of our lives. As we discussed in The Mind section, in much earlier centuries, stress occurred when life-threatening situations were actually happening. A lion or a bear would be running after you and you would need your fight or flight reaction to escape with your life. Your sympathetic nervous system turns on blood flows to your muscles; your analytical brain shuts off and you turn your attention to your body to find safety. You turn off the immune system, your digestive system, your repair and regeneration hormones and your actions are driven by your stress hormones to maximize survival. When the stress is gone, you turn off the adrenaline and the excitable sympathetic nervous system and go back into balance.

In our current setting, there are no lions, but rather ongoing stressors: traffic, coworkers, time pressures, financial pressure, divorce, family upsets, continuing irritations, anger, resentments, and hurt. We learn to live with elevated levels of stress hormones that cause disease. Research suggests that a large portion of office visits to the doctor are directly related to stress overload. Five out of six of the major causes of death in the United States are related to stress. If stress shuts off the immune system, it is no surprise that we get more infections and cancers. Stress shuts off the digestive system so it is no surprise that we get all kinds of digestive disturbances. Stress reduces our repair and regeneration system, so it is no surprise that healing slows down. Stress hormones raise blood pressure and encourage artery clogging.

In quantum mechanical terminology, we make ourselves a particle at the effect of other particles in our environment. We lose our creativity to create our future. The more we fall into this overstimulation for survival, the less freedom we have to use our own creative consciousness to create our lives.

According to quantum mechanics, the wave nature of reality is a realm of all possibilities. Creative potential is unlimited when energy is a wave. Only after it becomes a particle does it coalesce into a localized form. An electron as a wave is unlimited in its freedom to move and go in any direction without limitation in the field of all possibilities. When it is stressed into becoming a particle, for example, when a scientist attempts to measure it, its movement becomes limited and we then know with certainty about its movement. In terms of relationships, this means you see your partner as a limited, restricted personality who falls short of your expectations. You cannot see their unlimited nature which is hiding from your need to localize them.

Although these conceptions were developed from the world of science and its focus on subatomic particles, these ideas are startling and relevant to human life and relationships. The descriptions in physics mirror what we have seen in medical and therapeutic practices. In the world of scientific research, we have this "annoying" placebo effect where approximately 15 percent to a high 79 percent of the therapeutic effect of any medicine can be attributed to the placebo effect.[12] This means that the individual's belief that a treatment or medicine is going to help them actually impacts the benefits of any medicine or treatment.

In the practice of psychiatry, we consistently find that the approved FDA medicines for depression and other psychiatric disorders can improve symptoms by 35 percent to 40 percent. At the same time, the placebo effect is 30 percent.[13] This occurs because the beliefs that are held by the human mind are incredibly important to our health. When we allow ourselves to be in our wavelike nature and we believe in an unknown future, in this example, we believe that we can be helped by some medicine, we gain great health value from that medicine.

When we lose belief in our unknown but possible future, we shut off an important effect. We see this happening with the diagnosis of illnesses like cancer which, when presented as a certainty to a patient, can have devastating effects on their ability to heal from that illness.

Quantum mechanics describes that the reality of the physical world is coalesced wave energy. Let us look at modern science's understanding of physical reality. For thousands of years in human history since Aristotle, the physical world was thought to be eternal. Time and space were thought to be eternal and unchanging. Now, since the 1960s, science has discovered that time is changeable. Space is changeable. The physical world is not infinite. Rather it was created some 13 billion years ago according to science and it is expanding. This means that the physical universe is not fixed but rather continuously in the process of creation, just as we are!

Are we at the mercy of outside influences as the sympathetic nervous system stimulation would lead us to believe? Are we emotional victims of outside events? The Newtonian worldview that began in the 1700s implied that if we knew all the information about particles and objects (i.e., their masses, their momentum and their direction) we can then predict the future of all events. This is a matter-based perspective of the universe. It has certainly given us practical tools to deal with the material reality around us, but it is not the whole story of how life works.

This materialistic perspective limits us and puts us at the mercy of the events around us and takes away the thrill and creativity of engaging an unknown and uncertain future with new thoughts and resources. An unknown future offers us the freedom and joy of creating our future rather than the belief that we are limited by the material events in our life.

Are We Stuck as Victims of Our Past?

Quantum mechanics describes that when an observer is looking at a photon of light to localize its position or behavior, the photon changes from a wave to a particle. When the observer ceases observing, the particle returns back to a non-localized wave. Indeed, the attention of our consciousness affects the quantum mechanical reality of the wave/particle dynamic.

Our ability to love is directly related to our ability to move into our wave-like nature. For example, when we hold a newborn baby and look at their face, our heart swells with love. Why? It is because we allow ourselves to feel the fresh, unknown possibility that exists with this newborn child. We are not being a scientist who is trying to gain "objective" certainty about the baby. Rather, by connecting to the unknown field of all possibilities, our heart naturally swells. We connect to our wave-like nature and we experience deep love for the unlimited possibilities of the baby.

Any time we interpret another person as limited or as a certain limited way of being, we contract ourselves into our particle-like nature. The person we are perceiving in a limited way may react as a particle also, but they may not. Every person is free to react as a particle or wave. Unlike a photon or electron, a human always has a choice to experience themselves as a particle or a wave. We can choose how we experience our world and all the events in it.

When we get caught up in the past and experience stress and contract ourselves and become a particle and at the mercy of our interpretation of the event, love and connection disappears. When we feel our romantic partner is a certain way that we don't like and this thought brings back memories of past upsets, love begins to fade. Only by letting go of past upsets and allowing ourselves to move into the realm of the unknown future of all possibilities, can we rekindle the passion of romantic love.

Our consciousness is not passive but actually affects the physical An example from modern science is research about a programmed computer robot that moves randomly across a room. Then, as part of the experiment, the scientists have baby chicks born in that room. The chicks get attached to the moving robot as if it is their mother. Baby chicks will attach to the first thing it sees that is moving and that becomes its emotional mother forever. When the chicks, in this experiment, are then confined to one corner of the room, they cry out to the robot as if it is their mother. The research shows that the robot, then, responds to the chicks and spends the vast majority of its time in the part of the room near the chicks. This is chick consciousness affecting computer machinery. Consciousness is influencing what we think are random, mechanical events.[14]

In our romantic relationships, we can enhance the responsiveness of our partner and bring our partner emotionally closer by sending out thoughts of love and caring. We recommend not to hold back on thoughts and behaviors that express love and appreciation.

We can imagine that if one partner in a romantic couple has fears about abandonment, insecurities about infidelity, those thoughts that dominate their mind can actually push their partner away. Our consciousness can create our lives for harmony or conflict.

Behaviors are very important, but so are our thoughts. Thinking positive, uplifting thoughts and speaking positively about our future and ourselves and our romantic partner is essential. This is the basis of positive affirmations as a technology to move our lives forward into a magnificent future. It is important to make affirmations with strong beliefs and strong emotions to create connection like the chicks influencing the robot.

I advise you not to rely on your physician's confidence that this pill is going to make your life better. Rather, empower your doctor's recommendations by using the mental technology to influence your surroundings by your own conscious energy. I suggest two different approaches to activate consciousness to unfold your life into a magnificent future. The first technology is meditation. The second technology is learning to forgive everyone in your life.

QUESTIONS TO PONDER:

- *Are you allowing the past to restrict your possible future? Are fears and old hurts blocking your ability to create a magnificent future?*

CHAPTER 18

Meditation:
A TECHNOLOGY TO EXPERIENCE YOUR TRUE INNER SELF

We explored how consciousness is the fundamental reality that underlies our created world and that physical reality is a temporary coalescence of unbounded energy. We now know scientifically that $E=mc^2$, that is to say, energy is mass times the speed of light squared. All matter is nothing but energy concentrated into an apparent localized form we know as matter. With the understanding of quantum mechanics, we have learned that electrons can go back and forth from particles of matter to waves.

In our own lives we are responsible for moving back and forth between experiencing ourselves and others as a particle or wave. We have seen how the placebo effect is a respectable part of any medicine or medical treatment for illness. The material effect of a medicine is only a part of its benefits as we can enhance its effect by our beliefs about its effectiveness. Thus, our strong emotional beliefs and desires can affect our health, our environment and others in it. We have seen examples of how the strong desire of baby chicks to be close to their "robot" mother can affect the behavior of a computerized robot. Just like the baby chicks, our beliefs and emotions can have a direct effect on our physical world.

In addition, we understand that our physical wellness can be impacted by a buildup of stress in our physical body. Just as we can affect others and our environment by our strong thoughts, emotions and beliefs, we have an even greater impact on our own physical wellness. Our hormones, our brains, via the autonomic nervous system, sets the balance in our bodies. We can be stressed out or stress free.

Let us look at how we can contact this inner dimension and refocus ourselves away from outer things, objects, people, and time, as well as feelings and thoughts. This offers us the opportunity to be free from the material world. An inward focus invites us to move into the realm of our inner, unbounded self. This is how we can enjoy the pure experience of being a wave, rather than a particle. Our inner, unlimited self has the potential of enormous creativity that can be brought into our daily lives. Meditation is a methodology by which an individual can transcend the experience of thoughts and emotions and thereby change their physiology and their experience of themselves.

There are hundreds of research studies on the effects of meditation. My work as a doctor and my experience as a teacher of meditation come together to support my approach to staying healthy. I have seen thousands of people gain profound benefits from the practice of meditation. I have taught meditation to many thousands of people since 1973. Meditation is foundational to balancing hormones, as well as balancing and creating coherent brain waves. Meditation is critical to turning off the ongoing stress response that dominates our modern life. We all know how great it feels to go away on vacation for 10 days. We feel rejuvenated, calm and peaceful, ready to come back into our lives and jump into the creative activity that we love. Does it make sense that it is in our best interest to feel that way all the time?

Research (see Appendix) on meditation has overwhelmingly proven its value in promoting longevity, health and vitality, creativity, and harmonious relationship behavior. Feeling loving naturally comes when your body and mind are peaceful and balanced. It is so much easier to be loving to those around you when you are feeling rested and centered in your physical body. You can use the intellect to try and behave lovingly, but people around you can tell when you're tired and struggling to be loving.

Meditation is a process that allows you to experience your highest spiritual identity and to live from the deepest vision for your life. When you are stuck in the upsets of daily life, trapped in the hurts and fear and anger that comes up, you are restricted in how loving and visionary you can be. Later in this section of the book, we will show you how to apply the volumes of research on meditation and experience the deep rest and connection to your wave nature. This experience allows for the enhanced development you want and need to support the expansion of your heart and mind. This is a powerful technology for harmonizing brain waves, normalizing hormones, and improving your emotional well-being so that you can be an individual whose heart overflows with love.

The meditation process that I teach is effortless but also deep. I invite you to experience meditation through my online recording. You can access my guided meditation with the link: www.agelesslovebook.com/resources.

After the initial experiences in meditation there will be many questions that arise which are addressed in my book: *Secrets to Deep and Effortless Meditation*. This book on meditation will guide you through these experiences. My process of meditation has been refined over 40 years and taught to thousands of participants. The process of meditation that I teach is guaranteed to open you to uncovering the innermost nature of your own self.

My meditation process will allow you to contact the part of yourself that is beyond the emotional or physical pain that you may have experienced in the past. It can provide the passion for creating a future based upon your inspiration rather than a future based upon your past. As you experience that your inner self is filled with great joy and peace, you can begin to build a passion for living a life filled with love, joy and deep connection to a reality that is far beyond the physical world that supports you living the life you love with those you love.

As you recall how it felt when you first fell in love with your romantic partner, it was a time of openness to an unknown future. This felt expansive and happy. Meditation is a daily experience of that contact with the unknown and expansive future. Through meditation you will feel centered and open to appreciating your partner. Your heart will feel soft, loving and deeply accepting of yourself and your partner in all the quirky ways that make up your personalities.

Meditation is not just a spiritual practice. It is a physiological practice that changes the way our body and mind functions. Everyone can learn meditation no matter what your age. I have seen that it improves people's lives dramatically over time.

I have taught meditation to many couples. Consistently after some months of meditating the couples report that they are more calm, and have more patience and appreciation towards each other. They feel more inner contentment and it's easier to express loving words and behaviors. Love seems to radiate from them automatically after regular meditation.

With regular meditation the physical world can become just one possible reality, and a shallower reality than the world of possible futures that you can create. Meditation allows you to experience yourself free from physical and material reality. This is your contact with the quantum field. Along with joy and bliss comes motivation to use the power of your highest intentions to re-create your interpretations of your past and the wisdom to step into a new future. This daily practice supports your behavior as a wave.

QUESTION TO PONDER:

- *If you were more wave-like, how would it enrich your romantic partnership?*

CHAPTER 19

Experiences in Meditation:
TRANSFORMING OUR EXPERIENCE OF OUR "SELF"

When we are in our wave-like nature, we can see our partner as an unlocalized being of incredible qualities and potentials. If we see them as known particles of limited qualities, for example, as too sensitive, too critical, set in their ways, too emotional, too detached etc., we limit our vision of them and we create by our consciousness what we criticize. In the field of consciousness, what we resist persists in our experience. When we accept what our life is, we can transcend the limitations. Remember the tree and the metal fence that the tree expanded past as it took it into itself.

The great value of meditation is that the process allows us to become familiar with our wave-like consciousness and we can then integrate it into our lives. The basic experience in meditation involves letting go of your awareness of being in a body, letting go of your senses, letting go of your emotions, and gradually thoughts quiet down and you are left awake inside without any thought content. This involves a change in the brain waves, without falling asleep. This experience can be described as pure consciousness or experiencing the quality of "endless nothing." This experience in the beginning may be unclear or foggy, but after a while it will become familiar. It is deeply refreshing and rejuvenating, and comes with the feeling of inner happiness and joy.

When I teach meditation, you receive specific instructions that allow this process to occur easily and effortlessly. Fighting with the mind to quiet down is very unproductive. Being neutral about thoughts that come and go is an essential guideline. I have taught thousands of people to meditate and everyone can learn very easily as the structure of the human nervous system is wired to allow this process to occur.

A great value of meditation is the ability to retrain your physiology to experience a deep calm and peaceful state. The state of rest during meditation is generally 20 percent more than the deepest state of sleep. The deep rest of meditation is important to dissolve stress and imbalances in the physiology. Modern life is filled with so much stress from rushing around, worrying, interpersonal misunderstanding, juggling responsibilities, etc.

Sleeping is the usual way of dissolving stress. After a good night's sleep, we feel refreshed and able to start our day feeling better. The rest you gain from meditation is much deeper and the kind of stress we dissolve is much deeper. In the section on the body, we discussed how important it is to have a balanced physiology.

Meditation, however, is much more than just a stress release process. It is a process whereby you experience a deeper part of yourself. We can all contact the part of ourselves that is eternal, immortal and deeply peaceful through the process of meditation. This changes our experience of who and what we call our "self."

When we meditate, we experience that we are much more than our body, our senses, our emotions and our thoughts. We experience directly that what we are in essence is unbounded awareness, pure consciousness, "endless nothing," and endless peace and joy. This is an actual experience. It is not an intellectual idea. This experience comes along with feeling refreshed and rejuvenated, but it is much more than that.

After some time of meditating, the experience becomes very familiar and you may be able to have some thought activity while experiencing this inner expanded awareness. This quiet awareness can stay with you during the day when your eyes are open, and you feel a quality of joy and peace that permeates all your activity. Over a long period of time of regular meditating, you can experience that the peace of meditation stays with you throughout the day. This makes living and responding as a wave much easier.

The inner joy and peace that you experience becomes much greater than any outer activity that may have previously caused you irritation and annoyance etc. Now, activity seems to flow right through you without interrupting your peace.

Feeling more and more joy and peace during your day can be interrupted by your own thoughts and old habits and bring you out of this peaceful state. Past hurts, upsets, resentments, and anger can overshadow your awareness of bliss.

The more you live in this peaceful state, the more dramatic and upsetting it is to be thrown out of peace by past patterns of reacting to events in your life. We all have habits that have become automatic when certain events upset us. We carry them as a burden; we may call these experiences resentments or trauma. These burdens seem so real to us and they affect our interpretations of what is happening in the present.

There are two ongoing growth processes that are part of creating spiritual enlightenment. The first is described as the direct experience that your true self is your unbounded, unlimited, pure consciousness and you directly experience that this is who you are in meditation. The second aspect is bringing the unbounded, pure consciousness into the physical realm to live it and make it real in your daily life.

QUESTIONS TO PONDER:

- *Are you open to experience unbounded pure awareness deep inside your own consciousness?*
- *What would such an experience mean to you?*

CHAPTER 20

Research on Meditation:
TECHNOLOGY TO MOVE INTO OUR WAVE-LIKE NATURE

Medical research on meditation is voluminous. (See Appendix.) There are many different types of meditation and each one has value. Some types are easier to learn, but they all have benefits. Meditation lowers blood pressure significantly in meditators. There is a reduction of heart attacks and reduction of clogging of the arteries and less strokes. There is enhanced immune system functioning with less infections and less hospitalizations. Practitioners experience improvement in mood, depression, and anxiety.

Sleep disorders improve. Creativity improves. We have already discussed that the rest of meditation is twice as deep as sleeping. Along with this, one of the most dramatic changes in the physiology of meditators is brain wave changes. We see changes that have never been seen before on EEGs (Electroencephalogram). Brain waves become coherent, orderly and harmonious. This occurs both in the front and back, and right and left sides of the brain. These harmonious brain waves are correlated with the feeling of bliss and expanded awareness.

Clearly, meditation is not creating a mood, but rather training your body to move into a new physiological state that sends signals through the body to restructure your genetic expression and rebalance your hormones and sympathetic and parasympathetic nervous systems. As mentioned before, modern life has trained our bodies to live in a state of anxiety, stress, and irritability. We now have the opportunity to retrain our bodies to experience joy, peace and increase the experience of love that radiates from our heart.

Meditation allows us physiologically to feel more love independent of what particular events are going on in our life. This comes from creating harmonious coherent brain waves and sending hormones and nerve signals throughout our body that structures this new physiology. We are in charge of our responses. We are not dependent upon any particular outer experience to create positive, loving behavior.

The movement to feeling more love can be understood as moving into your wave nature. Another way of saying this is you are moving into the field of all possibilities as a conscious awareness. This is experienced as a fulfilling quietness that allows you to reach a state of deep peace.

This is foundational to restore love in your romantic relationship as love begins to overflow from your open heart. You cannot help but feel love toward your romantic partner when you are connected to a oneness in the realm of unbounded awareness. This experience brings into reality all of the possibilities that we've talked about in this book. It is what enables authentic ageless love.

Now we will look at how to integrate this meditation experience and make it an ongoing experience throughout our daily life when our eyes are open. Meditation is the foundational practice to change your physiology, your brain waves, and your experience of your own self. Meditation, however, is only 30 to 60 minutes a day. We need a spiritual practice for the rest of our waking time to support experiencing our life from our wave nature.

The quantum understanding of life is that this whole physical universe is energy that only appears as particles. This more complete understanding of life invites us to live as an unbounded awareness, as a wave, that can never be fully localized as a certainty. On the quantum level, science tells us, you can never know the position and momentum of any particle. There is a quality of uncertainty that always exists. With this comes the ability to create your own future.

The Path of Spiritual Growth: Moving Our Wave-Like Nature into Our Relationship

The process of integrating the experience in meditation into the physical realm and living it 24/7 can be accomplished in either one of two general paths of personal relationship.

One possible path is having a teacher-mentor or personal spiritual advisor. This spiritual mentor will guide you, press you, and push you to do things that generally you would not think of doing but it will help you to grow and develop beyond your own personal ego. It is not designed to be fun or easy. I know people who have been on this path and it is challenging.

The other path is the path of romantic married life. This path is more common in our western culture. We all know many who follow this path. It also is not designed to be fun and easy. A romantic relationship presses you and pushes you to develop yourself and grow beyond your pain and fear and resentments. Spiritual enlightenment requires that you let go of all emotional upsets from the past. Ultimately, for the deepest peace and connection to the unbounded quantum field, you will want and need to see your past as the perfect journey that allowed you to grow and fulfill your purpose in this life.

QUESTION TO PONDER:

- *Are you willing to devote 30 minutes a day to develop the experience of an inner self filled with peace?*

CHAPTER 21

The Foundation of Ageless Love:

CONSCIOUSLY LETTING GO OF THE PAST AND LIVING INTO THE FUTURE

In The Mind section of our *Ageless Love* book, we concluded that only by seeing our partner as a wave, a non-local, unknown and mysterious being, can we fully appreciate and enjoy ageless love. When we see our partner as a particle, a person with a fixed reality, with known and unchangeable qualities, we lose the experience of feeling like we are "in love."

In our personal lives, we interpret experiences and make them into a fixed reality that frames our future experience. Imagine a married individual, Joe, who has been hurt in the past by his parents' divorce. Now, Joe lives in fear that his spouse may leave him or be unfaithful. We can see how these fears can shape Joe's emotional life and push away his spouse by his accusations and insecurities as Joe constantly suspects infidelity. Thus, Joe creates his own worst future. Joe is living as a particle with his fears, worries and anxiety and experiences his partner as a particle. Thus, falling in love forever is out of Joe's realm.

We all do this to some extent. Meditation is a very helpful practice for learning how to let go of the need to have certainty in our life.

We all intend to be our best selves with those we love. We try to be conscious and do the right thing. However, that abstract goal is difficult to maintain amidst the challenges of life. When we are stressed with the busyness of our lives, we become imbalanced in our hormones and emotionally and physically tired, we lose the feeling of enthusiasm about our life and our relationships, and our behavior does not match our ideal values.

Meditation Allows us to Dissolve Stress

Meditation opens us to the direct experience of the realm of "endless nothing" that we come to know as the innermost experience of our self. Mental clarity as well as physical and emotional health require us to learn to be open and comfortable with this creative and unknown realm of all possibilities and its uncertainty.

This energy for creativity invites us to fulfill our vision for a future that requires applying our talents and interests to create that future. The creativity from pure consciousness is available when we let go of the hurts, resentments, fears, and overall complaints about past events in our life. This is not a small goal but rather a process over time.

We all go through difficult experiences growing into maturity. In The Mind section we outlined the spiral of development where we can recreate ourselves through the lifecycle. Advancing to higher stages requires us to accept our past and take responsibility for creating our future. As we grow into higher stages of development we see the past has given us our purpose and enhanced our wisdom of life. As we let go of our story about our suffering, we experience our true self.

Meditation is a process that supports this movement. This growth also requires our intellect and our passion to keep us focused and moving towards a future we create. The future is an unknown, but we can give direction to this unknown. Holding on to past pain is nonproductive. Each one of us can go through a process where we give up the thoughts, fears, resentments, and shame that cause us to live as a particle.

When you let go of the emotional requirement that things have to be a certain way, you can still prefer that it be the way you want without holding on to the emotional upset. Allow yourself to move back into your wave-like nature and forgive the other person. Let go of the anger, the resentment, the hurt, and fear that stops you from moving into your wavelike nature. This will bring you joy and peace.

As you learn to do this more and more with small events in your daily life, you will find that you can let go of upsets more easily. More and more you live in the pure awareness of joy and peace that comes from meditation. It will stick with you throughout your day.

Little by little you will allow the right side of your brain to connect you to the infinite, unbounded awareness. This experience will grow and become a daily reality. The passion will become more and more intense to live in this wave of freedom. Giving up insistent thoughts that things have to be a certain way will become your new normal.

You will naturally make up interpretations of events that bring you peace rather than upsets that push you into your particle-like nature. For example, a driver cuts you off on the freeway and speeds off. Instead of getting upset and angry you can think, "I hope they get to the hospital in time before the baby is born." You don't know for sure why they are speeding, so why not make up a thought that brings you peace?

All of our interpretations are just made up. We don't know the ultimate meaning of any event until our life is over and we have a chance to review it from the perspective of the higher heavenly realms when we see the big picture of our life on this earth.

Each of us has work to do in giving up our complaints in life. Often, there is one overriding complaint that shapes our personality and casts a shadow over our relationships. This complaint is one that we can begin to work on once we have attained some skill in letting go of our little upsets. Having life complaints that predictably constrain us and contract us into being particle-like, is likely based on very real traumas or emotions that are not easily or instantly dismissed.

Let me share my experience of letting go of the past, my story of hurts, and complaints about my life. I want each of you to be inspired to look at your life story and see the hurt and complaints you want to give up.

My Path to Love: Transforming Wounds into Gifts

I remember when Barbara and I were having a lot of problems and thinking about divorce. I was in my 30s and filled with emotional pain as Barbara was complaining and unhappy. We were stuck. We had many counsellors and I even went to a psychic.

The psychic said, "Yes, you will separate and divorce, but it will be for good and you will have a good life."

My response was intense: I said to myself, *"Who do you think you are telling me what my future is? I have young children and I'm not divorcing, and I will make this dysfunctional marriage work and I am going to turn myself inside out until I do. Nobody is going to tell me that my future is set."* My passion for a future where I recreate my marriage with my wife became intense and I was willing to go to whatever classes, courses, and mentors I needed to assist me to change myself in whatever ways were needed.

Barbara encouraged me to take a variety of personal growth classes with her. Left to myself, I would not have done any of those things. But with her encouragement and my desire to make the marriage work, I followed her suggestions. There were many mentors that came into my life. They pressed and pushed me to look at my complaints about life and the hurts from my childhood.

Let me describe these hurts and complaints. Although I had a truly loving family life, my inner experience of my Mom was that she was hard to please and often angry. As a child my mom was strict and I complained she did not appreciate me enough and was too hard in criticizing me. Let me share one intense memory about this that occurred when I was about eight years old.

My mom would come home with my dad from work in the family store at 7:30 PM and she expected her three boys to not make a mess in the house. On one occasion I remember trying so hard to be neat. I had everything cleaned up and tried to leave nothing out of place. I was using one glass to drink tap water. I left the glass in the sink and used the same glass over and over placing it back into the sink carefully.

When my mom and dad came home, my mom was angry that I could not wash the one glass I used. She screamed at me that I, "was ungrateful for all her hard work and left the glass in the sink unwashed." I was devastated. She hollered at me for what seemed like one hour about my ungratefulness. My childhood memories were a collection of hurts about how my Mom did not appreciate my efforts to please her.

My childhood showed up as an unsuccessful effort to please my mom. Topping off that collection of hurts was having my mom come to my high school graduation. It was my big hope of pleasing my mom with my accomplishments. Out of a graduating class of 1,000 students, the top 25 children got called up on the stage to receive an award. Most of the 25 top students received one award and occasionally someone got two awards. I received 7 awards, tied with the valedictorian. I expected an enthusiastic acknowledgement of my great achievement.

What I received from my mom afterwards was: "I expect you to do well." My heart popped like a balloon breaking. It was a very devastating experience. I felt I could never please my mother. I kind of gave up on pleasing her.

When I was 17 years old my mom was angry at her three boys and spoke to us very little for one year because we forgot her birthday card. Indeed I had such good reasons for my life complaint.

Overall through my late 30s, I had a general complaint about life: "My mom does not think I am good enough." This colored my whole outlook on life. My personality was structured to try to show the world I am so good that everyone will like me and word will get back to mom that I am really great. For example, I have focused on being the best doctor. This had the effect of making me the greatly beloved doctor to many, but consequently shortchanged my wife and children from my time and attention.

Each of us in our own lives can become aware that our complaints about our life can also create positive effects in our life. However, carrying around that emotional baggage will also have negative consequences.

When I was about 35 years old, and trying to save my marriage, I had a revelation with the assistance of mentors and personal growth courses that Barbara encouraged me to attend. I realized *I needed to give up my desire to have my mom ever think I am good enough*

My big complaint was standing in the way of creating my life as I wanted it to be: I want to radiate the love and wisdom of God into this physical plane. It was a strange experience giving up that complaint as it had become such a deep part of my personality.

My belief that my mom did not think I was good enough had led me to withhold my love and appreciation of my mom and it kept me complaining about all the women in my life, especially my wife, who also, in my mind, did not appreciate me enough. Any semblance of criticism from my wife would set off past memories and hurt from my childhood.

What I learned about myself was that underneath the hurt from Barbara's complaints about how I was not an emotionally or even physically present husband, was my longstanding resentment that my mother's complaints about me in my childhood were completely unfair. The pain from my mom's relentless criticism echoed in my heart when Barbara complained about anything and inferred I didn't care about her. I could not hear her. This was a replay of my mom's misjudgment of me. I reacted by tightening up and defending myself as though my life was at stake. I spent years as a particle in those conversations and this did not move us forward as a couple.

Eventually, I was able to step away from my interpretation. It helped me see my mom differently. I saw how much she loved me and how much she loved the family. What surprised me about my breakthrough was how much I cried. The tears seemed endless. Underneath my resentment with my mom was my hurt that she didn't truly know me when I was a teen. And, her misconceptions about me were not flattering. This new understanding and release of hurt and anger opened my heart towards my mom and Barbara.

I want everyone who reads this book to gain the perspective that your future is open to all possibilities when you let go of your resentments and commit to growing your life. Letting go of your stories about how your life is controlled by other people who have hurt you is the bridge that brings you to the awareness that you are responsible for creating your life. This is an essential element in becoming a Stage 5 Wise Elder.

Nobody knows your future. You create your own future right now. The spiral diagram of the stages of growth illustrates the levels of growth that are open to each of us. It is not designed to be easy and smooth, but rather it requires commitment to grow and learn. It takes a bigger perspective and awareness along with letting go of your old way of seeing things to create a new future.

Meditation will be a big part of opening your awareness to new perspectives and a new future. Meditation will naturally dissolve stresses that have accumulated in your physiology. Nevertheless, your intellect is a very important part of your willingness to let go of the past.

You can choose to change your thoughts, your beliefs, your emotions. It takes a strong desire and willingness to give up anger, fear, and resentment, etc. By giving up these restricted emotions, we open ourselves to unlimited possibilities to create the future we desire.

As a contrast to my story, another story allows me to show you what unresolved feelings and negative beliefs can do to constrict us and move us down a contracted path where we live life as a particle and struggle.

This strangely clarifying story is a Buddhist tale called, "The Lost Son".

This is a story about a widower father who lost his beloved five-year-old son. While away on a business trip, robbers came and burned down his village, and took his son away. When the father returned, he mistook the burnt remains of an infant to be his son. He was uncontrollably sad. He collected the ashes of his son and carried them around in a bag on his back continuously. Some weeks later his real son escaped from the bandits and found his way home.

When he arrived at his father's rebuilt home at midnight, he knocked on the door. His father thought, "Who is knocking on my door at midnight?" When the child answered, "It's me Papa, open the door," his father was in a confused state and still deeply mourning. He was angry and thinking that some other child was making fun of him. The father shouted, "Go away." The son cried out more, but the father could only mourn for his son and screamed, "Go away." After a time, the child left. Father and son never saw each other again.

This parable is a thoughtful story that dramatizes how our interpretations and fixed beliefs about the past can sabotage the opportunity of the future. These beliefs trap us in a future that is filled with unnecessary suffering.

Like the father in the parable of the lost son, the heavy burden I carried around with me for many years into my 30s was that my mother did not love, acknowledge, and appreciate all my efforts to please her as a child and teenager. My memories were filled with so many stories that reinforced my beliefs and feelings.

We all do this to some degree or another as a child. We have memories that prove our hurt feelings tell the truth. Of course, as a parent with our own children, we know that being a perfect parent is an impossible task.

The heavy burden I carried about my mother not loving me enough, not appreciating me, or acknowledging me for all the things I did for her was in fact keeping me from experiencing the kind of life that I desired. In fact, it was an excuse for my unloving behavior with my wife and other personal relationships.

The release of my hurt and anger at being misunderstood as a child and the acceptance of all that happened in the past opened my heart to loving my mother and provided me with the breakthrough of loving my wife the way she wanted to be loved. It was a miracle that can be understood and reproduced by anyone who is motivated to end their victimhood and create a new future.

Each of us have many complaints in our life that we use as our reasons why our life is not providing us with what we want. These complaints can lead to anger, sadness, disappointment, regret, shame, guilt, resentments, etc. Spiritual growth requires us to let go of the past and live into a future which we consciously create. A lovely story that I heard on a spiritual retreat deeply moved me. It clarifies how it feels to move through the stages of spiritual growth.

A little girl of 5 saw a plastic necklace in a store and asked her mom if she could get it. Her mom said it was expensive and would cost one month's allowance. The little girl was happy to forgo her allowance for one month. She wore the necklace day and night for one year.

Her father, who would read to her each night, said after one year, "Sweetheart, Daddy would really like your necklace. Would you give it to Daddy?" The little girl replied, "Oh Daddy, please not my necklace. Here, why don't you take my teddy bear; I love my teddy bear." Her Dad said OK.

The next night her father said, "Sweetheart, I really would like you to give me your necklace." She said: "Oh no Daddy, please not my necklace; here, take my lovely giraffe, I love my giraffe." Daddy said, "OK."

After many nights of asking, the little girl finally cries and says, "OK Daddy, you can have my necklace." He takes it from her and then he reaches into his pocket and takes out the most exquisite white pearl necklace and gives it to his daughter.

As this parable describes, as each of us becomes willing to give up our plastic necklace which is the story of our childhood and past resentments, complaints, hurt, shame, etc., we will receive a gift that is immeasurably more valuable, more lovely, more fulfilling. We will experience an infinite, unbounded, fulfilling future that comes from giving up our particle nature and living into our wave-like nature.

Our wave-like nature is not localized, but filled with all possibilities. These possibilities arise from our new self which we directly experience from meditation and from our heart's freedom from the bondage to our interpretations which restrict us from feeling intense, personal love. We do not know the intensity of joy and fulfillment that is available to us until we let go of the limitation we place on ourselves.

Letting go of these limitations appears difficult, but it is the door that opens to incredible fulfillment. The intensity of love for our romantic partner is limited when we hold on to our plastic necklaces and, like the parable of the lost son, hold on to our grief and suffering.

My decision to reject the "known" future pronounced by the psychic, when I was thinking of divorce, represented my giving up my plastic necklace and my new willingness to accept the metal fence in my life and grow beyond my own personal limitations. As I reflect on my path, it is clear to me that the intensity of my emotional commitment to turn myself inside out, as needed, to recreate my relationship with Barbara, pushed me and pressed me to grow in ways I would not have done if left on my own. Clearly my commitment to making my romantic life work with Barbara was the motivating energy that pressed me to grow past my complaints about the women in my life. Barbara was also the moving force to support and coach me to share deeply with my dad which was life-changing for me when he was passing away from lung cancer and I was 36 years old.

Our relationship with our romantic partner will often be the energy that presses us to grow in ways we would not pursue on our own. This is the blessing and the opportunity of romantic love over a lifetime. I want this for each of you in your own lives.

By being open to giving up all your hurts, resentments, withholds, anger etc., you can create your own incredible future where you feel loved, appreciated and respected beyond your wildest expectations. Your romantic partnership will allow you, if you are open to your wave-like nature, to create a magnificent future.

What do you need to shift from seeing your world as a particle, to now experience your life as a wave? What holds you back from the kind of future you want for yourself?

It takes letting go of the past and releasing yourself from seeing the events of your life as limitations. Recall the tree metaphor that I described in the introduction to The Spirit section.

The metal fence protected the baby tree, but became a limitation when the tree matured. This is a metaphor for all of our past experiences that seem to hold us back in the present. My mother's toughness as a parent prepared me and pressed me to accomplish much in this lifetime. Like the tree, I learned to embrace the metal fence (my mother) and grow beyond and appreciate her.

What we interpret as limitations, once had a great value to support us in our growth process. Every childhood is filled with complaints about parents. Almost nobody has "perfect" parents. And the few individuals I have met who think their parents were perfect may be so satisfied with themselves that they lack aspiration in life.

However, accepting the metal fences in our life requires us to experience the world around us as a wave and not as a particle that bounces into us and hurts us and limits us. We can learn to accept all these events by not resisting them or complaining about them, but rather by reinterpreting them from a bigger perspective. Like the tree, we can open ourselves to our wave nature and encompass the metal fence into our very being. Then we can grow beyond the apparent limitations in our life.

For me, as a young man invested in my logical mind, I needed to grow in the realm of expanding my heart. This required me to accept myself and to accept Barbara as very different from me. This process is inevitable in any long-term relationship over a period of many years.

Growing and changing is the nature of life. This is one of the messages of the spiral of development diagram. The intensity of joy and peace becomes increasingly concentrated as you move to the highest levels of human development. I am so grateful for all the experiences that have brought me to this loving and creative time in life.

We all can do this. It takes passion and commitment to create your own future. You can change your physiology, your genetic programming, your personality, and transform your experience of being an individual and a partner in an endlessly loving relationship. Amazingly, my wife thinks I am God's gift to her. I feel blessed by God every day as showers of love come to me in waves throughout the day. I feel it in my meditations and when my eyes are open.

We want everyone who reads this book to experience an inner knowing that they can recreate their lives to be truly magnificent. No one needs to be a victim of past or present events that occur in the physical world. Each of us are unbounded beings with the God-given inner consciousness that is creative.

QUESTIONS TO PONDER:

- *What are the plastic necklaces that you might be living with?*
- *Are you willing to give them up for beautiful pearls?*

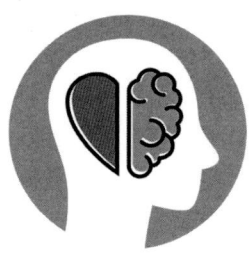

CHAPTER 22

Epilogue

Do You Want to Live as a Particle or a Wave?

Let's review: the quantum field is the field of all possibilities, where creation comes from. The act of observing the electron or photon causes the wave nature of the photon or electron to turn into a particle.

What does this mean? This means our attention is powerful. It means that maybe we don't have to work so hard to create. Perhaps there is another way to create besides putting pressure on matter.

Since the 1800s with Newton, Darwin and others, we have been taught to become the object of nature, a more sophisticated animal. Meanwhile, our culture has drifted into an emphasis on materialism. This was the first scientific revolution. Since then, as a culture, we have become more left brain dominant. We want to know for certain, while the right brain is more integrative, more comfortable with mystery and the unknown.

Now, ultimately, we need both sides of the brain. The holistic right brain is a balance for the orderly, strategic left brain. Together they allow us to see paradoxes. Together, they contribute their respective strengths by navigating our lives towards wholeness as well as accomplishment. So, we are not disrespectful of the left brain. However, quantum theory invites us to balance our brains in our personality and create not from effort but by intention. It means we need to learn to contact the quantum field which is everywhere.

The question, "Do you want to live as a particle or wave" is tongue-in-cheek. As a particle you are matter, you are a thing, and you're stuck with your interpretations of cause and effect in the world. "She hurt me." "He betrayed me." You can move your life forward as a particle, but it is a lot of work!

As a wave, you participate in creation and move your life forward by thought, intention and prayer. Meditation and forgiveness and a loving heart has the potential for connecting us to the quantum field, and each other. Too much left-brain has given us a secular and mechanistic society. The correction is coming with the quantum field.

With the prescriptions that we offer in this book, each person can take steps that will free them from their hurt and disappointments, and feelings of victimization. Each person can transform their lives by acting on these prescriptions that promote living in the world as an unbounded being who creates their own lives.

Meditation will allow you to experience that happiness comes from inside you and is not based upon outside experiences. Past experiences that have been a burden to you emotionally and physically can be resolved and reinterpreted as learning experiences that have brought you more in touch with your own unbounded self.

Use the prescriptions in our book as action steps to transform your lives into the experience of ageless love.

Prescriptions for the Spirit
PRACTICES TO LIVE IN THE FIELD OF ALL POSSIBILITIES

Rx #1: Learn deep, effortless meditation.

Struggle less, enjoy more: Link to Dr. Grossman's meditation sessions: **www.agelesslovebook.com/resources**

Rx #2: Allow meditation bliss to direct your future

Allow the magnificent, infinite, blissful selfhood you experience in meditation to be the energy that directs you into your future self now. Commit to daily meditation practice. You can change your physiology, your genetic programming, your personality, and transform your experience of being an individual and a partner in an endlessly loving relationship.

Rx #3: Giving up your complaints

Recognize that you have complaints that limit your life and realize you need to give these up so that you can live into your magnificent future. Make a list of complaints you have about others in your life.

Rx #4: Forgive everyone; write a love letter

Begin your healing with the process of forgiving everyone in the past that you think may have hurt you intentionally or unintentionally.

Write a letter to each person forgiving them but don't actually send the letter.

The letter is for you to clarify your thoughts and resolve your feelings.

Use the "Love Letter" technique, popularized by John Gray, author of many books on relationships.

It is common to get stuck in one of the emotions, such as anger, sadness, or fear. Therefore, please spend equal time in each of the feeling sentences because the purpose of writing the letter is for you to work through the full range of your emotions.

There are generally four layers of feelings that are blocking the path to love and acceptance:

- *Anger and Blame.* Start your letter with a paragraph that begins, "Dear _____ ," and complete the following sentences.

    I don't like it when . . .

    I hate it when . . .

    I resent . . .

    I'm fed up with . . .

    I am tired of . . .

    I want . . .

- *Sadness and Hurt.* Next, write a paragraph that completes these sentences.

    I feel hurt when . . .

    I feel disappointed because . . .

    I feel sad when . . .

>   I feel hurt when . . .
>
>   I want . . .

- *Fear and Insecurity.* Next, write a paragraph that completes these sentences.

  >   I'm afraid that . . .
  >
  >   I feel scared because . . .
  >
  >   I'm worried that . . .
  >
  >   I do not want . . .
  >
  >   I need . . .
  >
  >   I want . . .

- *Guilt, Regret, and Responsibility.* Now take responsibility for your part in the upset.

  >   I'm sorry that . . .
  >
  >   I feel embarrassed . . .
  >
  >   I'm sorry for . . .
  >
  >   Please forgive me for . . .
  >
  >   I didn't want . . .
  >
  >   I want . . .

- *Intention and Wishes.*

  >   I want . . .
  >
  >   I wish . . .
  >
  >   I hope . . .

- *Love and Acceptance.*

  I forgive you for . . .

  Thank you for . . .

  I Love . . .

  I want . . .

  I understand . . .

  I appreciate . . .

  I know . . .

The love letter process can help you resolve old hurts and feel better within a very short time.

Do not give the letter to the intended recipient. The letter is a private venting designed to express and resolve your own feelings.

- *Write down how this forgiveness is changing your life.*
- *See and feel this change as present and real right now.*
- *Create a positive affirmation . . .* "I am living in joy and peace as I forgive . . . I wish them love and all good things."

Rx #5: Take our workshop, Falling in Love Forever

You will learn skills to allow you to be a wave in your romantic relationship. You will grow in love and understanding and unfold your spiritual growth.

Go to **www.agelesslovebook.com/resources**

Mythologist Joseph Campbell says: "Marriage is not a love affair; it is an ordeal." We believe your relationship is your own personalized program of self-development, and a perennial training ground for working together in love and partnership. Our workshop grows your personality, opens you to healing childhood injuries, strengthens your partnership communication, and intensifies feelings of being appreciated and respected.

All of this is essential to achieving ageless love. Developing your ability to see your partner as the unbounded, limitless wave they are, rather than a fixed entity, takes practice, focus and understanding.

We have designed a workshop that will guide you in creating ageless love and in forging a deeper connection with your partner to unlock the passion and love you desire. Our workshop will open you to live a romantic relationship filled with joy and wisdom. We want all this for you.

Appendices

APPENDIX #1:
STUDIES ON BIO-IDENTICAL HORMONE BENEFITS

A Comprehensive Review of the Safety and Efficacy of Bioidentical Hormones for the Management of Menopause and Related Health Risks
Alternative Medicine Review Volume 11, Number 3 September 2006:208-223
Deborah Moskowitz, ND

Conclusion: The studies reviewed suggest bioidentical progesterone does not have a negative effect on blood lipids or vasculature as do many synthetic progestins, and may carry less risk with respect to breast cancer incidence. Studies of both bioidentical estrogens and progesterone suggest a reduced risk of blood clots compared to non-bioidentical preparations.

Bioidentical hormone preparations have demonstrated effectiveness in addressing menopausal symptoms.

There is currently sufficient evidence to support their preferred use over that of their synthetic cousins.

The bioidentical hormone debate: are bioidentical hormones (estradiol, estriol, and progesterone) safer or more efficacious than commonly used synthetic versions in hormone replacement therapy?
Kent Holtorf; Postgrad Med. 2009 Jan;121(1):73-85.

Conclusion: Physiological data and clinical outcomes demonstrate that bioidentical hormones are associated with lower risks, including the risk of breast cancer and cardiovascular disease, and are more efficacious than their synthetic and animal-derived counterparts. Until evidence is found to the contrary, bioidentical hormones remain the preferred method of HRT.

Progesterone vs. synthetic progestins and the risk of breast cancer: a systematic review and meta-analysis.
Noor Asi,: Syst Rev. 2016; 5: 121.

Results: Studies enrolled 86,881 postmenopausal women with mean age of 59 years and follow-up range from 3 to 20 years. Progesterone was associated with lower breast cancer risk compared to synthetic progestins when each is given in combination with estrogen.

Conclusion: Observational studies suggest that in menopausal women, estrogen and progesterone use may be associated with lower breast cancer risk compared to synthetic progestin.

Point/Counterpoint: The Case for Bioidentical Hormones.
Steven F. Hotze, M.D., Donald P. Ellsworth, M.D.; Journal of American Physicians and Surgeons; Volume 13; Number 2 Summer 2008

Conclusion: The use of exogenous chemicals as hormone substitutes has been shown to be unsafe and should be stopped. Hormone supplementation should be done with compounds identical to the natural molecules. Although more research is needed, there is already evidence of the benefits of hormone supplementation in the proper doses and in proper balance. The future of medicine is in physiology rather than pharmacology.

Effects of estradiol with micronized progesterone or medroxyprogesterone acetate on risk markers for breast cancer in postmenopausal monkeys.
Wood, C., et al.; Breast Cancer Res Treat. 2007; 101: 125-134.

Results: The addition of the synthetic progestin medroxyprogesterone acetate (MPA) to postmenopausal estrogen therapy significantly increases breast cancer.

Conclusion: These findings suggest that oral micronized progesterone has a more favorable effect on risk biomarkers for postmenopausal breast cancer than medroxyprogesterone acetate.

Bioidentical, Synthetic, and Animal Based Hormone Replacement Therapies and Risk of Breast Cancer.
Abenhaim, Haim Arie MD; Obstetrics & Gynecology: May 2017 - Volume 129 - Issue 5 - p S132.

Conclusion: While HRT (Hormone Replacement Therapy) use is associated with an overall increased risk of breast cancer, this association appears to be unique in women having been given synthetic progestogens. Synthetic progestogens should not be given as part of HRT and counseling regarding the risk of breast cancer should consider the effect of formulation used.

Topical Progesterone Cream Does Not Increase Thrombotic and Inflammatory Factors in Postmenopausal Women.
Blood (ASH Annual Meeting Abstracts). 2004; 104: Abstract Stephenson, K., Price, c., et al

Comparison of Regimens Containing Oral Micronized Progesterone or Medroxyprogesterone Acetate (Provera) on Quality of Life in Postmenopausal Women: A Cross-Sectional Survey.
J Women's Health Gender Based Med. 2000; 9 (4): 381-387.
Fitzpatrick, L.A., M.D., Pace, c., BS, Wiita, B., Ph.D

A cross-sectional survey was conducted to examine quality of life (QOL) related to physiological, somatic, and vasomotor effects of changing progestogen treatment from medroxyprogesterone acetate (MPA) to micronized progesterone in postmenopausal women.

Conclusion: When compared with the MPA-(Provera) containing regimen, women using micronized progesterone-containing HRT experienced significant improvement in vasomotor symptoms, somatic complaints, and anxiety and depressive symptoms. Women reported improved perceptions of their patterns of vaginal bleeding and control of menopausal symptoms while on the micronized progesterone-containing regimen. Approximately 80% of women reported overall satisfaction with the micronized progesterone-containing regimen. A micronized progesterone-containing HRT regimen offers the potential for improved QOL as measured by improvement of menopause-associated symptoms.

Cardiovascular Benefits

Hum Reprod. 2006; 21 (10): 2715-2720.
Differential effects of oral conjugated equine (Premarin) estrogens and transdermal estrogen on atherosclerotic vascular disease (ASVD) risk markers and endothelial function in healthy postmenopausal women.
Yen-Ping Ho, 1., et al.

Background: Recent studies have revealed that Hormone Replacement Therapy (HRT) may increase the risk for atherosclerotic vascular disease (ASVD).

Methods: We investigated the effects of HRT via different administration routes on the markers for ASVD and endothelial function in healthy postmenopausal women.

Conclusion: These data suggest that oral estrogen induces ASVD risk by increasing acute inflammation; however, transdermal estrogen avoids this untoward effect. Additionally, transdermal estrogen exerts a positive effect on endothelial function similar to that of oral estrogen. Therefore, the transdermal route might be favorable in terms of ASVD risks.

Circulation. 2007; 115: 840-845.
Hormone Therapy and Venous Thromboembolism Among Postmenopausal Women. Impact of the Route of Estrogen Administration and Progestogens: The ESTHER Study
Canonico, M., et al.

Background: Oral estrogen therapy increases the risk of venous thromboembolism (VTE) in postmenopausal women. Transdermal estrogen may be safer. However, currently available data have limited the ability to investigate the wide variety of types of progestogens.

Conclusions: Oral but not transdermal estrogen is associated with an increased venous thromboembolism (VTE) risk. In addition, our data suggest that norpregnane derivatives (provera) may be thrombogenic, whereas micronized progesterone appears safe with respect to thrombotic risk. If confirmed, these findings could benefit women in the management of their menopausal symptoms with respect to the VTE risk associated with oral estrogen and use of progestogens.

Vaginal Health

NEJM. 1993; 329 (11): 753-756.
A Controlled Trial of Intravaginal Estriol in Postmenopausal Women with Recurrent Urinary Tract Infection
Raz, P., Stamm, W.E.

Background: Recurrent urinary tract infections are a problem for many postmenopausal women.

Conclusion: The intravaginal administration of estriol prevents recurrent urinary tract infections in postmenopausal women, probably by modifying the vaginal flora.

Psychiatry

Arch Gen Psychiatry. 2005; 62: 154-162.
Dehydroepiandrosterone Monotherapy in Midlife-Onset Major and Minor Depression
Schmidt, P., Daly, R.

Conclusion: We find DHEA to be an effective treatment for midlife-onset major and minor depression.

Bone Health and Testosterone in Women

Maturitas. 1995; 21(3): 227-236.
Testosterone Enhances Estradiol's Effects on Postmenopausal Bone Density and Sexuality

Davis, S.R., McCloud, P., et. al.
We concluded that in postmenopausal women, treatment with combined estradiol and testosterone implants was more effective in increasing bone mineral density in the hip and lumbar spine than estradiol implants alone. Significantly greater improvement in sexuality was observed with combined therapy, verifying the therapeutic value of testosterone implants for diminished libido in postmenopausal women. The favorable estrogenic effects on lipids were preserved in women treated with Testosterone, in association with beneficial changes in body composition.

Testosterone Replacement in Men

Testosterone Therapy and Cardiovascular (CV) Risk: Advances and Controversies
Abraham Morgentaler, MD;
Mayo Clin Proc. February 2015;90(2):224-251

Conclusion: Review of the literature clearly reveals a strong relationship between higher serum Testosterone (T) concentrations, endogenous or via T therapy, as beneficial for reduction of CV disease and CV risk factors. Public health may be harmed not only by inadequate appreciation of an actual risk but also by the failure to offer beneficial treatment for a medical condition because of false claims of risk concerns. On the basis of the current state of evidence, placing restrictions on the appropriate use of T therapy for T-deficient men is likely to result in compromise of public health and a substantially increased future financial burden on the US healthcare system.

In summary, we find no scientific basis for the suggestion that T therapy increases CV risk. In fact, as of this date, we are unaware of any compelling evidence that T therapy is associated with increased CV risk. On the contrary, the weight of evidence accumulated by researchers around the world over several decades clearly indicates that higher levels of T are associated with amelioration of CV risk factors and reduced risk of mortality.

Am J Mens Health published online 20 February 2014
Jeannie J. Su, Samuel K. Park and T. Mike Hsieh

The Effect of Testosterone on Cardiovascular (CV) Disease: A Critical Review of the Literature
Review of modern literature suggests a CV -protective effect of Testosterone (T) in men. Emerging data have begun to shed light on the mechanism of action of androgens on the CV system. T therapy can reverse symptoms of hypogonadism while potentially reducing CVD risk factors.

Osukui PM et al. *Testosterone and the cardiovascular system: a comprehensive review of the clinical literature.*
J Am Heart Assoc. 2013 Nov 15;2(6) (Excellent literature review)

Conclusion: Low T associated with mortality, more CVD, higher intimal artery thickness (early artery disease), more coronary spasm.

Ohlsson et al. **High serum testosterone is associated with reduced risk of cardiovascular events in elderly men. The MrOS study in Sweden.** Journal of the American College of Cardiology. Oct 11 2011;58(16):1674-1681.
Study had four quartiles of serum testosterone:>550
- 439 – 550
- 341 – 438
- <340
- Only the top quartile showed 30% less CV events
- Any of the lower quartiles showed increased events

Conclusion: This supports the idea that optimal Testosterone is over 500.

Testosterone and Mortality Vakkat Muraleedharan, T. Hugh Jones; Clin Endocrinol. 2014;81(4):477-487.

Conclusions of this 10 page review article: Testosterone deficiency may have an adverse effect on general health. Testosterone deficiency is associated with a poorer quality of life, reduced physical strength and muscle bulk, fatigue, mood changes including lack of motivation, poor concentration and depression and that there may be an impairment of the immune system. These clinical parameters potentially would add to earlier mortality.

Men with higher endogenous testosterone levels have less cardiovascular events.

APPENDIX #2:
MALE ERECTILE DYSFUNCTION

Shock Wave Therapy (Gainswave) For Erectile Dysfunction
Clinical Trial BJU Int. 2015 Apr;115 Suppl 5:46-9.

Evaluation of clinical efficacy, safety and patient satisfaction rate after low-intensity extracorporeal shockwave therapy for the treatment of male erectile dysfunction: an Australian first open-label single-arm prospective clinical trial.
Eric Chung 1, Ross Cartmill

Objective: To evaluate the efficacy, safety and patient satisfaction rate with low-intensity extracorporeal shockwave therapy (LiESWT) in Australian men with erectile dysfunction (ED), as LiESWT induces neovascularization and potentially enhances penile perfusion and improves erectile function.

Patients and methods: Open-label single-arm prospective study of patients with ED with five-item versions of the International Index of Erectile Function (IIEF-5) scores of >12 at baseline were enrolled after informed consent. Patient demographics, change in IIEF-5 and Erectile Dysfunction Inventory of Treatment Satisfaction (EDITS) scores, and overall satisfaction score (on a 5-point scale) were recorded. Treatment consists of 3000 shockwaves (1000 shockwaves to the distal penis, base of penis and corporal bodies at the perineum) twice weekly for 6 weeks.

Results: All patients had tried and failed oral phosphodiesterase type 5 inhibitors and most of the patients had ED for >18 months [mean (range) 21.8 (6-60) months]. No side-effects to LiESWT were reported. Most patients reported an improvement in IIEF-5 score by 5 points (60%) and EDITS Index score by >50% (70%). Most patients were satisfied (scoring 4 out of 5; 67%) and would recommend the therapy to their friends (80%).

Conclusion: LiESWT appears to improve erectile function, is safe and potentially plays an important role in penile rehabilitation in men who failed medical therapy.

Gainswave (Extracorporeal Shock Therapy) ReviewArticle
Eur Urol. 2017 Feb;71(2):223-233.
Low-intensity Extracorporeal Shockwave Treatment Improves Erectile Function: A Systematic Review and Meta-analysis
Zhihua Lu

Context: As a novel therapeutic method for erectile dysfunction (ED), low-intensity extracorporeal shock wave treatment (LI-ESWT) has been applied recently in the clinical setting. We feel that a summary of the current literature and a systematic review to evaluate the therapeutic efficacy of LI-ESWT for ED would be helpful for physicians who are interested in using this modality to treat patients with ED.

Objective: A systematic review of the evidence regarding LI-ESWT for patients with ED was undertaken with a meta-analysis to identify the efficacy of the treatment modality.

Evidence acquisition: A comprehensive search of the PubMed and Embase databases to November 2015 was performed. Studies reporting on patients with ED treated with LI-ESWT were included. The International Index of Erectile Function (IIEF) and the Erection Hardness Score (EHS) were the most commonly used tools to evaluate the therapeutic efficacy of LI-ESWT.

Evidence synthesis: There were 14 studies including 833 patients from 2005 to 2015. Seven studies were randomized controlled trials (RCTs); however, in these studies, the setup parameters of LI-ESWT and the protocols of treatment were variable. The meta-analysis revealed that LI-ESWT could significantly improve IIEF (mean difference: 2.00; 95% confidence interval [CI], 0.99-3.00; $p<0.0001$) and EHS (risk difference: 0.16; 95% CI, 0.04-0.29; $p=0.01$). Therapeutic efficacy could last at least 3 mo. The patients with mild-moderate ED had better therapeutic efficacy after treatment than patients with more severe ED or comorbidities. Energy flux density, number of shockwaves per treatment, and duration of LI-ESWT treatment were closely related to clinical outcome, especially regarding IIEF improvement.

Conclusions: The number of studies of LI-ESWT for ED have increased dramatically in recent years. Most of these studies presented encouraging results, regardless of variation in LI-ESWT setup parameters or treatment protocols. These studies suggest that LI-ESWT could significantly improve the IIEF and EHS of ED patients. The publication of robust evidence from additional RCTs and longer-term follow-up would provide more confidence regarding use of LI-ESWT for ED patients.

We reviewed 14 studies of men who received low-intensity extracorporeal shockwave treatment (LI-ESWT) for erectile dysfunction (ED). There was evidence that these men experienced improvements in their ED following LI-ESWT.

Five-year study on extracorporeal shockwave therapy
Sex Med. 2021 Aug;9(4):100384.
Evaluation of Long-Term Clinical Outcomes and Patient Satisfaction Rate Following Low Intensity Shockwave Therapy in Men With Erectile Dysfunction: A Minimum 5-Year Follow-Up on a Prospective Open-Label Single-Arm Clinical Study
Eric Chung 1, Ross Cartmill 2

Introduction: Low intensity extracorporeal shockwave therapy (LIESWT) improves erectile function (EF) in men with vascular erectile dysfunction (ED) but longer-term outcomes remain unknown.

Aim: To evaluate the clinical outcomes of LIESWT at a minimum 5-year follow-up.

Methods: This is an open-label single-arm prospective study involving men with vascular ED who received LIESWT.

Main outcome measure: Changes in patient demographics, IIEF-5 and Erectile Dysfunction Inventory of Treatment Satisfaction (EDITS) scores, as well as overall satisfaction score (on a 5-point scale) were reviewed at 12, 24, 48, and 60 months after completion of LIESWT. A chi-square contingency analysis was used to examine the relationship between erectile function score and treatment satisfaction, with statistical significance set at 5%.

Results: The mean follow-up period was 69.9 (63-82; median 76) months. The mean IIEF-5 scores for pretreatment and after treatment at 12, 24, 48, and 60 months were 14.8, 17.6, 16.8, 16.5, and 16.5 while the percentages of patients who reported an improvement in IIEF-5 score by five points were 60%, 45%, 40%, and 40%; and EDITS scores >50% were recorded in 70%, 55%, 50%, and 48% of patients at 12, 24, 48, and 60 months post-LIESWT. Ten patients required medical therapy and two patients opted for penile prosthesis implantation. The overall satisfaction rate appeared in sustained subsequent follow-up (score 4 out of 5; 68% vs 50% vs 40% vs 40% at 12, 24, 48, and 60 months). There were minor time-limited incidents, but no significant adverse event reported.

Conclusion: This long-term study showed the observed clinical improvement in EF continues to deteriorate but appears to plateau at 40% clinical efficacy at 48-60 months after completion of LIESWT. The absence of penile pain and deformity at 5-year follow-up supports the long-term safety data of LIESWT in men with ED.

Platelet-Rich Plasma & Erectile Dysfunction

Randomized Controlled Trial J Sex Med. 2021 May;18(5):926-935
Platelet-Rich Plasma (PRP) Improves Erectile Function: A Double-Blind, Randomized, Placebo-Controlled Clinical Trial
Evangelos Poulios

Background: Animal studies postulate that platelet-rich plasma (PRP) injections improve key elements of the pathophysiologic mechanisms leading to erectile dysfunction (ED).

Aim: To conduct the first double-blind, randomized, placebo-controlled trial assessing the efficacy and safety of PRP injections in patients with mild and moderate ED.

Methods: Sixty sexually active patients with mild and moderate ED were randomly assigned to two sessions, with a one-month difference, of 10 mL PRP (n = 30) or placebo (n = 30) intracavernosal injections. An FDA-approved separation system was used. Patients were evaluated at 1, 3 and 6 months after completion of the treatment protocol. A per-protocol analysis was applied. All participants withheld any ED treatment during the trial.

Outcomes: The achievement of minimal clinically important difference (MCID) in the International Index of Erectile Function - Erectile Domain (IIEF-EF) from baseline to six months after final treatment. Erectile function at all time points, as well as safety of PRP injections, were also evaluated.

Results: At 6 months, a MCID was achieved by 20/29 (69%) patients in the PRP group compared to 7/26 (27%) in the placebo group. The risk difference between the two groups was 42% (95%CI: 18-66), $P < 0.001$ and the baseline-adjusted mean between-group-difference in the IIEF-EF score was 3.9 points (95%CI: 1.8-5.9). Similarly, a statistically significant difference of both the number of participants attaining a MCID and the IIEF-EF score was also observed at the 1- and 3-month evaluation between the two groups. Accordingly, patients receiving PRP were more satisfied with the treatment. No adverse events were observed during the study period.

Clinical implications: Intracavernosal PRP injection therapy used as outlined in this trial appears to be a safe and effective short-term treatment for the management of mild to moderate ED.

Strengths & limitations: We conducted the first clinical trial exploring the role of PRP in the management of ED. Conversely, our findings lack external validity due to single-center design.

Furthermore, our results cannot be extrapolated to other PRP separation systems.

Conclusions: PRP intracavernosal injections may be a promising addition to the urologist's armamentarium for the management of ED.

Erectile dysfunction and Platelet-Rich Plasma & Cell Therapy Review Article:

Prog Urol. 2020 Dec;30(16):1000-1013.
Biotherapies for erectile dysfunction and Peyronie's disease: Where are we now?
[Article in French] W Akakpo

Introduction: Clinical trials of cell therapy for erectile dysfunction (ED) and Peyronie's disease (PD) were recently conducted after preclinical studies.

Aims: The aims of this study are to give an update on biotherapy for ED and PD and to describe the regulatory framework for these therapies.

Materials and methods: A literature review was performed through PubMed and Clinical.trials.gov addressing cell therapy for ED and PD and using the following keywords "erectile dysfunction," "Peyronie's disease," "stem cell," and "platelet-rich plasma."

Results: Preclinical studies in rodent models have shown the potential benefit of cell therapy for ED after radical prostatectomy or caused by metabolic diseases, and PD. The tissues used to obtain the therapeutic product were bone marrow, adipose tissue and blood (PRP, platelet-rich plasma). Mechanism of action was shown to be temporary and mainly paracrine.

Four clinical trials were published concerning ED after radical prostatectomy and in diabetic patients and one for PD. Eleven clinical trials including 3 randomized trials are currently going on. Preclinical and preliminary clinical results suggested the possibility to improve spontaneous erectile function and response to pharmaceutical treatment in initially non-responder patients. This effect is mediated by an improvement of penile vascularization. A reduction of penile curvature without side effects was noted after injections into the plaque of PD patients.

Most of these therapeutic strategies using autologous cells were considered as "Advanced Therapy Medicinal Products" with strict regulatory frameworks imposing heavy constraints, in particular in case of "substantial" modification of the cells. The regulatory framework remains unclear and more permissive for PRP and cell therapy processes with **extemporaneous preparation/injection and no "substantial" modifications.**

Conclusions: First results on cell therapy for ED and PD are promising. The regulatory framework can significantly change according to cell preparations and origins leading to various constraints. This regulatory framework is crucial to consider for the choice of the procedure.

APPENDIX #3:
FEMALE SEXUAL DYSFUNCTION AND PLATELET-RICH PLASMA

Turk J Obstet Gynecol. 2019 Dec;16(4):228-234.
Platelet-rich plasma administration to the lower anterior vaginal wall to improve female sexuality satisfaction
Gökmen Sukgen

Objective: To investigate the effect of platelet-rich plasma (PRP) injection to the lower one-third of the anterior vaginal wall on sexual function, orgasm, and genital perception in women with sexual dysfunction.

Materials and methods: Four sessions of PRP were administered to the anterior vaginal wall of 52 female patients with sexual dysfunction and orgasmic disorder [Female Sexual Function Index (FSFI) total score ≤26 orgasmic subdomain score ≤3.75]. Prior to the PRP administrations in each session, the FSFI validated in Turkish, the Female Genital Self-Image Scale (FGSIS), the Female Sexual Distress Scale-Revised (FSDS-R), and Rosenberg's Self-Esteem Scale were used and in the final follow-up, and the Patient Global Impression of Improvement (PGI-I) was performed and the results were analyzed.

Results: Following the application of the PRP, the total FSFI score was observed as 27.88±4.80 and the total score was 26 and above in 50% of the patients ($p<0.001$). Orgasm subdomain scores were found as 2.11±1.20 before the PRP treatment and 4.48±1.14 afterwards ($p<0.001$). A significant change was observed in all sub-domains after PRP and it was observed that this change started after the first administration ($p<0.001$). A statistically significant increase was determined in FGSIS genital perception scores, which was significant between the 1st and 2nd months ($p<0.001$). The FSDS-R scores showed a minimal increase in stress scores as the application number increased, but a statistically significant decrease was observed in the 4th administration (p<0.001). No statistically significant difference was found in Rosenberg Scale scores before and after treatment (p=0.389). High satisfaction was found in PGI-I scores.

Conclusion: As a minimally invasive method, PRP administration to the distal anterior vaginal wall may improve female sexuality with high satisfaction.

Menopause. 2018 Oct;25(10):1124-1130.

Efficacy of injecting platelet concentrate combined with hyaluronic acid for the treatment of vulvovaginal atrophy in postmenopausal women with history of breast cancer: a phase 2 pilot study
Barbara Hersant

Objective: Approximately 50% to 70% of breast cancer survivors are affected by one or more symptoms of vulvovaginal atrophy (VVA). For those who cannot take hormone therapy, autologous platelet-rich plasma combined with hyaluronic acid (A-PRP-HA) may provide a new alternative therapy for the treatment of VVA in postmenopausal women with history of breast cancer.

Methods: We enrolled 20 postmenopausal breast cancers survivors with VVA and a score of <15 on the Gloria Bachman Vaginal Health Index (VHI) comprised of five items including: vaginal pH, elasticity, fluid volume (secretions), epithelial integrity, and moisture. We administered intramucosal injections of A-PRP combined with HA (Regenkit) and performed clinical evaluations at 0, 1, 3, and 6 months. Primary endpoint: evaluation of vulvovaginal mucosa changes using the VHI; secondary endpoint: evaluation of dyspareunia and sexual dysfunction based on the Female Sexual Distress (FSD) score.

Results: All participants (20 women) showed improvement in the clinical symptoms of vaginal dryness and dyspareunia. The VHI score showed a significant increase at 6 months, going from a total baseline score (pretreatment) of 10.7 ± 2.12 to 20.75 ± 4.8 (P < 0.0001) at 6 months. Improvement in hydration and vaginal epithelial integrity was reported. A VHI score of > 15 showed a successful treatment outcome. The FSD score decreased significantly during the study, from a baseline score of 36.35 ± 2.53 pretreatment to 30.15 ± 2.47 6 months after treatment, representing improvement of 17% ($P < 0.0001$, respectively). No adverse events were reported.

Conclusions: The injection of A-PRP-HA appeared to be a promising method to improve the trophicity and hydration of vaginal mucosa for the treatment of VVA in postmenopausal breast cancer survivors with contraindications to hormone therapy.

APPENDIX #4:
STEM CELLS AND ORTHOPEDICS

Berman et al. Int J Stem Cell Res Ther 2019, 6:064
Volume 6 | Issue 1
Prospective Study of Autologous Adipose Derived Stromal Vascular Fraction Containing Stem Cells for the Treatment of Knee Osteoarthritis
Mark Berman, MD, Elliot Lander, MD, Thomas Grogan, MD, Walter O'Brien, MD, Jonathan Braslow, MD, Shawntae Dowell and Sean Berman, MS

Background: The management of osteoarthritis of the knee runs the spectrum of care from a variety of conservative treatments often culminating in total joint arthroplasty.

We initiated a large prospective study to evaluate whether autologous adipose derived stromal vascular fraction (SVF -rich in stem cells) therapy is a safe and effective option.

Results: 2,586 patients were treated. Statistically significant improvement was seen at 1 and 2 years - meaningless pain and greater ease of mobility.(82% overall improvement).

Conclusion: Deployment of autologous SVF represents a simple surgical procedure that can be safely performed in an adequate outpatient environment under straight local anesthesia and demonstrates very good outcomes even in difficult cases of chronic knee arthritis.

Mesenchymal Stem Cell-Derived Exosomes for Effective Cartilage Tissue Repair and Treatment of Osteoarthritis
Young Guk Kim
Biotechnol J. 2020 Dec;15(12)

Recent studies have shown that the administration of MSC-exosome effectively reduced a production of inflammatory cytokines in chondrocytes, increased the expression of cartilage ECM component, and eventually augment cartilage tissue regeneration in a series of in vivo studies. Therefore, this review emphasizes current engineering approaches via MSC-exosome for cartilage tissue repair, as a functional OA treatment technique.

Cartilage Repair by Mesenchymal Stem Cell-Derived Exosomes: Preclinical and Clinical Trial Update and Perspectives
Leila Taghiyar
Adv Exp Med Biol. 2021;1326:73-93

Exosome vesicles (EV) are novel therapeutic approaches for treatment of cartilage lesions and OA. The results of recent studies have shown that EVs isolated from mesenchymal stem cells (MSCs) could inhibit OA progression. EVs isolated from various stem cell sources, such as MSCs, may contribute to tissue regeneration of the limbs, skin, heart, and other tissues.

APPENDIX #5:
MEDITATION RESEARCH ARTICLES

Meditation: Process and effects
Hari Sharma; Ayu. 2015 Jul-Sep; 36(3): 233–237.
(Great general review of meditation research)

Changes in genetic expression (epigenetics) in meditators

Medicina (Kaunas) 2021 Mar 1;57(3):218
Transcriptomics of Long-Term Meditation Practice: Evidence for Prevention or Reversal of Stress Effects Harmful to Health
Supaya Wenuganen

Background and objectives: Stress can overload adaptive mechanisms, leading to epigenetic effects harmful to health. Research on the reversal of these effects is in its infancy. Early results suggest some meditation techniques have health benefits that grow with repeated practice. This study focused on possible transcriptomic effects of 38 years of twice-daily Transcendental Meditation® (TM®) practice.

Materials and methods: First, using Illumina® BeadChip microarray technology, differences in global gene expression in peripheral blood mononuclear cells (PBMCs) were sought between healthy practitioners and tightly matched controls (n = 12, age 65). Second, these microarray results were verified on a subset of genes using quantitative polymerase chain reaction (qPCR) and were validated using qPCR in larger TM and control groups (n = 45, age 63). Bioinformatics investigation employed Ingenuity® Pathway Analysis (IPA®), DAVID, Genomatix, and R packages.

Results: The 200 genes and loci found to meet strict criteria for differential expression in the microarray experiment showed contrasting patterns of expression that distinguished the two groups.

Differential expression relating to immune function and energy efficiency were most apparent. In the TM group, relative to the control, all 49 genes associated with inflammation were downregulated, while genes associated with antiviral and antibody components of the defense response were upregulated. The largest expression differences were shown by six genes related to erythrocyte function that appeared to reflect a condition of lower energy efficiency in the control group. Results supporting these gene expression differences were obtained with qPCR-measured expression both in the well-matched microarray groups and in the larger, less well-matched groups.

Conclusions: These findings are consistent with predictions based on results from earlier randomized trials of meditation and may provide evidence for stress-related molecular mechanisms underlying reductions in anxiety, post-traumatic stress disorder (PTSD), cardiovascular disease (CVD), and other chronic disorders and diseases.

Lower Blood Pressure in Meditators

Am J Hypertens. 2009 Dec. 22(12):1326-31.
A randomized controlled trial on effects of the Transcendental Meditation program on blood pressure, psychological distress, and coping in young adults.
Sanford I Nidich

Background: Psychological distress contributes to the development of hypertension in young adults. This trial assessed the effects of a mind-body intervention on blood pressure (BP), psychological distress, and coping in college students.

Methods: This was a randomized control trial (RCT) of 298 university students randomly allocated to either the Transcendental Meditation (TM)program or wait-list control. At baseline and after 3 months, BP, psychological distress, and coping ability were assessed. A subgroup of 159 subjects at risk for hypertension was analyzed similarly.

Results: Changes in systolic BP (SBP)/diastolic BP (DBP) for the overall sample were -2.0/-1.2 mm Hg for the TM group compared to +0.4/+0.5 mm Hg for controls (P = 0.15, P = 0.15, respectively). Changes in SBP/DBP for the hypertension risk subgroup were -5.0/-2.8 mm Hg for the TM group compared to +1.3/+1.2 mm Hg for controls (P = 0.014, P = 0.028, respectively). Significant improvements were found in total psychological distress, anxiety, depression, anger/hostility, and coping (P values < 0.05). Changes in psychological distress and coping correlated with changes in SBP (P values < 0.05) and DBP (P values < 0.08).

Conclusions: This is the first RCT to demonstrate that a selected mind-body intervention, the TM program, decreased BP in association with decreased psychological distress, and increased coping in young adults at risk for hypertension. This mind-body program may reduce the risk for future development of hypertension in young adults.

Less Diabetes in Meditators

Int J Yoga.May-Aug 2018;11(2):122-128.
Effect of 6 Months of Meditation on Blood Sugar, Glycosylated Hemoglobin, and Insulin Levels in Patients of Coronary Artery Disease
Shashank Shekhar Sinha

Background and objectives: Coronary artery disease (CAD) is the leading cause of morbidity and mortality worldwide. It has been recognized that stress, diabetes, and hypertension are important in etiology and progression of CAD. This study is to evaluate the role of meditation in improving biochemical parameters such as blood glucose, glycosylated hemoglobin, and serum insulin levels in known CAD patients.

Material and methods: Sixty CAD patients are divided into two groups of which one group did meditation and other did not. Blood glucose, glycosylated hemoglobin, and fasting serum insulin levels were measured before and at the end of 6 months of study in both the groups.

Results: At the end of the study, significant decrease was seen in patients who practiced meditation as compared to other group.

Conclusion: Meditation may modulate the physiological response to stress through neurohumoral activation, which may be a novel therapeutic target for the treatment of CAD.

Telomeres (aging DNA) and Stress & Meditation

Randomized Controlled Trial Psychoneuroendocrinology.
2011 Jun;36(5):664-81.
Intensive meditation training, immune cell telomerase activity, and psychological mediators
Tonya L Jacobs

Background: Telomerase activity is a predictor of long-term cellular viability, which decreases with chronic psychological distress (Epel et al., 2004). Buddhist traditions claim that meditation decreases psychological distress and promotes well-being (e.g., Dalai Lama and Cutler, 2009). Therefore, we investigated the effects of a 3-month meditation retreat on telomerase activity and two major contributors to the experience of stress: Perceived Control (associated with decreased stress) and Neuroticism (associated with increased subjective distress). We used mediation models to test whether changes in Perceived Control and Neuroticism explained meditation retreat effects on telomerase activity. In addition, we investigated whether two qualities developed by meditative practice, increased Mindfulness and Purpose in Life, accounted for retreat-related changes in the two stress-related variables and in telomerase activity.

Methods: Retreat participants (n=30) meditated for ~6 h daily for 3 months and were compared with a wait-list control group (n=30) matched for age, sex, body mass index, and prior meditation experience. Retreat participants received instruction in concentrative meditation techniques and complementary practices used to cultivate benevolent states of mind (Wallace, 2006). Psychological measures were assessed pre- and post-retreat. Peripheral blood mononuclear cell samples were collected post- retreat for telomerase activity. Because there were clear, a priori hypotheses, 1-tailed significance criteria were used throughout.

Results: Telomerase activity was significantly greater in retreat participants than in controls at the end of the retreat ($p<0.05$). Increases in Perceived Control, decreases in Neuroticism, and increases in both Mindfulness and Purpose in Life were greater in the retreat group ($p<0.01$). Meditation analyses indicated that the effect of the retreat on telomerase was mediated by increased Perceived Control and decreased Neuroticism. In turn, changes in Perceived Control and Neuroticism were both partially mediated by increased Mindfulness and Purpose in Life. Additionally, increases in Purpose in Life directly mediated the telomerase group difference, whereas increases in Mindfulness did not.

Conclusions: This is the first study to link meditation and positive psychological change with telomerase activity. Although we did not measure baseline telomerase activity, the data suggest that increases in perceived control and decreases in negative affectivity contributed to an increase in telomerase activity, with implications for telomere length and immune cell longevity. Further, Purpose in Life is influenced by meditative practice and directly affects both perceived control and negative emotionality, affecting telomerase activity directly as well as indirectly.

J Tradit Complement Med. 2021 Feb 15;11(5):409-418.
Rapid changes of miRNAs-20, -30, -410, -515, -134, and -183 and telomerase with psychological activity: A one year study on the relaxation response and epistemological considerations
Carlo Dal Lin

Background and aim: Mental stress represents a pivotal factor in cardiovascular diseases. The mechanism by which stress produces its deleterious effects is still under study, but one of the most explored pathways is inflammation-aging and cell senescence. In this scenario, circulating microRNAs appear to be regulatory elements of the telomerase activity and alternative splicing within the nuclear factor kappa-light-chain-enhancer (NF-κB) network. Anti-stress techniques appeared to be able to slow down the inflammatory and aging processes. As we recently verified, the practice of the relaxation response (RR) counteracted psychological stress and determined favorable changes of the NF-κB, p53, and toll-like receptor-4 (TLR-4) gene expression and in neurotransmitters, hormones, cytokines, and inflammatory circulating microRNAs. We aimed to verify a possible change in the serum levels of six other microRNAs of cardiovascular interest, involved in cell senescence and in the NF-κB network (miRNAs -20, -30, -410, -515, -134, and -183), and tested the activity of telomerase in peripheral blood mononuclear cells (PBMCs).

Experimental procedure: We measured the aforementioned molecules in the serum of patients with ischemic heart disease (and healthy controls) immediately before and after a relaxation response session, three times (after the baseline), in one year of follow-up.

Results: According to our data, the (favorable) miRNA-20 and -30 levels and PBMCs-telomerase activity increased during the RR while the (deleterious bio-markers) -410 and -515 levels and miRNA-134 and -183 decreased.

Conclusion: The mediators considered in this exploratory work appeared to vary rapidly with the psychological activity (in particular when focused on relaxation techniques) showing that psychological activity should be part of the future research on epigenetics.

Brain Wave Changes In Meditation
Ann N Y Acad Sci. 2014 Jan;1307:1-8.

Transcendental experiences during meditation practice

Frederick Travis

This article explores transcendental experiences during meditation practice and the integration of transcendental experiences and the unfolding of higher states of consciousness with waking, dreaming, and sleeping. The subject/object relationship during transcendental experiences is characterized by the absence of time, space, and body sense--the framework that gives meaning to waking experiences. Physiologically, transcendental experiences during Transcendental Meditation practice are marked by slow inhalation, along with autonomic orientation at the onset of breath changes and heightened α1 (8-10 Hz) frontal coherence. The integration of transcendental experiences with waking, dreaming, and sleeping is also marked by distinct subjective and objective markers. This integrated state, called Cosmic Consciousness in the Vedic tradition, is subjectively marked by inner self-awareness coexisting with waking, sleeping, and dreaming. Physiologically, Cosmic Consciousness is marked by the coexistence of α1 electroencephalography (EEG) with delta EEG during deep sleep, and higher brain integration, greater emotional stability, and decreased anxiety during challenging tasks. Transcendental experiences may be the engine that fosters higher human development.

APPENDIX #6:
SCIENCE OF ORBITALS

Just as human life progresses from the coupling of a man and woman, so does the world of quantum mechanics progresses as electrons get paired and create the complex molecules of life.

O_2 is the chemical symbol for two oxygen atoms that come together to create one molecule of oxygen that makes up our atmosphere. They do this so each atom of the two oxygen atoms that make up the **oxygen molecule** can share two electrons with their partner atom. This allows the 2 oxygen atoms to share 4 electrons in their outer shell. Each oxygen atom is satisfied to have a total of 8 electrons in their outer shell (Figure 1.).

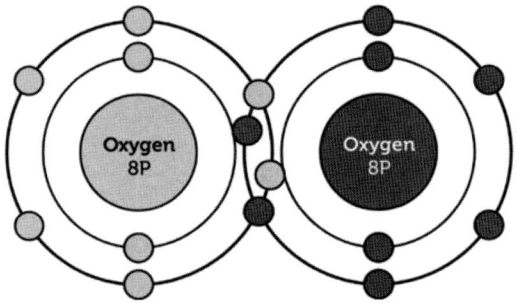

Figure 1.

Another example is H_2O, the chemical symbol of water. Two hydrogen atoms come together with one oxygen atom. Each hydrogen atom shares a single electron with the oxygen atom so that both oxygen and hydrogen atoms have fully paired electrons in their outer shells. Now each hydrogen atom (Figure 2.) has 2 electrons in the outer shell and the oxygen atom has 8 electrons in the outer shell. H_2O is one of the most common molecules in the universe.

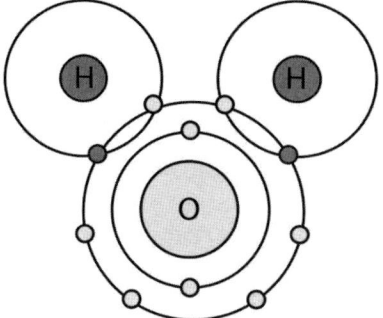

Figure 2.

The molecules of life will often contain carbon atoms that need to share 4 electrons in their outer shell to have fully paired electrons. This allows for long chains of carbon atoms to connect to many other atoms. This provides the molecules of life that have complex proteins where carbon pairs with oxygen, hydrogen and nitrogen or other atoms to create what is necessary for life. The very foundation of molecules in the universe is the pair bonding of electrons!

See below example of **glucose** (Figure 3.). Each carbon atom shares a single electron with 4 other atoms creating long complex chains of atoms that are required for life.

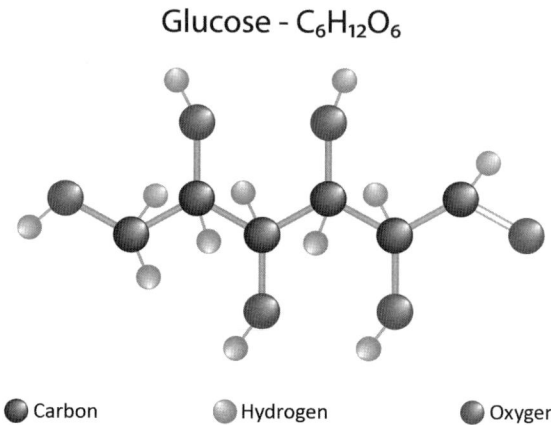

Figure 3.

Orbital Shapes

Just as human life grows and gets more complex as we mature and develop, so the electron orbits get increasingly more complex as the electrons gain energy. Remember each orbital can have 1 or 2 electrons, but no more than 2. Also, recall that electrons would normally repel each other because negative charged particles naturally push each other away like the same poles on a magnet. However, as long as the electrons have opposite spins, they can move in the same orbital.

Orbitals are a mathematical probability that an electron will be 90 to 95% of the time somewhere within the geometrical space of the orbital. However, you cannot really localize the electrons; you can only statistically say where they are generally moving as a wave at almost the speed of light.

Orbit one, the spherical **s orbital,** (Figure 4.), is closest to the nucleus of the atom. Each progressive energy level of the orbitals gets increasingly bigger and more distant from the nucleus, but also dramatically more complex.

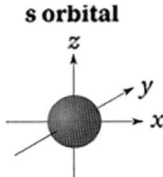

Figure 4.

The 1st closest orbit to the nucleus is round and simple.

Electrons may move in an electron pair in stable orbits for thousands or millions of years. When our universe was first formed it was made up entirely of the basic spherical s orbital of hydrogen and helium, atoms that only have one or two electrons. Over the millions of years as stars exploded, many more complex atoms with complex electron pairs were formed which now make up our earth.

APPENDIX #6 **187**

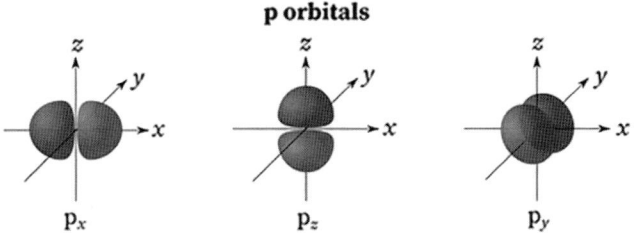

Figure 5.

The 2nd level of orbitals are called **p orbitals** (Figure 5.) and are more complex. There are 3 possible orbitals all of equal energy levels. Each orbital shape is like 2 dumbbells aligned to either the X, or Y, or Z axis. The likelihood that the electron will be moving in that region 90 to 95% of the time. Notice the alignments allow each of the different 3 orbitals to have minimal overlap with each other.

The 3rd level of orbitals is called **d orbitals** (Figure 6.). There are 5 possible d orbitals. They are even more complex. It becomes increasingly hard to visually see how each of these 5 different orbitals can have minimal overlapping with each other.

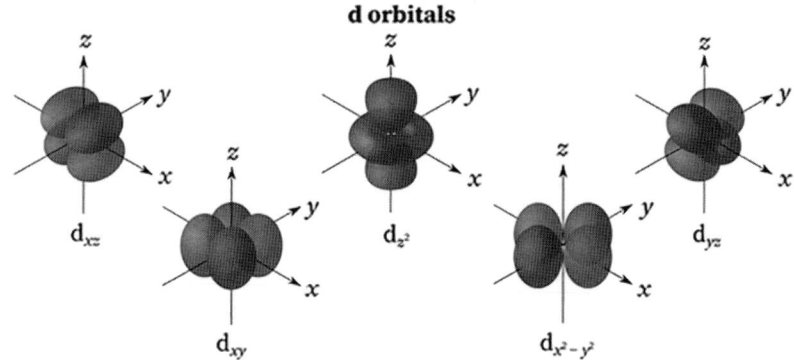

Figure 6.

The 4th level of energy orbitals are 7 possible **f orbitals** (see Figure 7.). They are ever farther out from the nucleus and dramatically more complex. It becomes almost impossible to visualize how each of these 7 orbitals can have minimal overlapping with each other. There are even more levels of orbitals but this gives you a good idea of how the electron pairs move in greater complexity as the energy levels of the orbits increase.

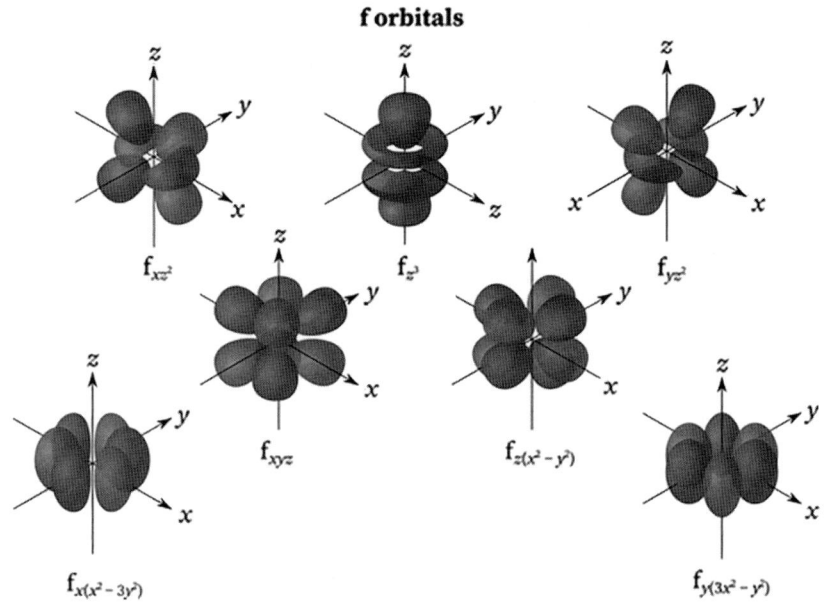

Figure 7.

These complex orbitals of higher energy levels are a metaphor for the consciousness of a 2-year-old compared to a 8-year-old; compared to a 14-year-old; compared to a 25-year-old; compared to a 50-year-old, etc.

APPENDIX #7:
RESOURCES FOR FINDING DOCTORS PRACTICING ANTI-AGING AND REGENERATIVE MEDICINE

For up-to-date list of physicians in your area, please go to:
www.agelesslovebook.com/resources

ENDNOTES

1. John Gottman, "*The Roles of Conflict Engagement, Escalation, and Avoidance in Marital Interaction: A Longitudinal View of Five Types of Couples,*" Journal of Consulting and Clinical Psychology, 1933. Vol. 61, No. 1.6-15.

2. See list of movies, e.g. *Gone with the Wind, Out of Africa, Ghost, Titanic, Casablanca, Romeo and Juliet*, etc.

3. McGilchrist, Iain, *The Master and His Emissary. The Divided Brain and the Making of the Western World.* New Haven: Yale University Press, 2009.

4. This study indicates that a diet of unlimited food intake including junk food and dairy products produce less healthy offspring for generations.

   Eur J Hum Genet. 2007 Jul;15(7):784-90.

   Transgenerational response to nutrition, early life circumstances and longevity.
   Gunnar Kaati 1, Lars Olov Bygren, Marcus Pembrey, Michael Sjöström

5. My Favorite supplement companies are Ortho Molecular, Designs For Health, Metagenics, NuMedica. These can be accessed through **www.agelesslovebook.com/resources.**

6. J Cardiovasc Pharmacol Ther. 2015 Jan;20(1):52-8.

   Effects of an oral nitric oxide supplement on functional capacity and blood pressure in adults with prehypertension.
   Olivia S Biswas
   Nitric oxide supplementation appears to lower blood pressure in patients with prehypertension and might be beneficial as a routine supplementation for cardiovascular protection.

7. Atherosclerosis. Volume 302, June 2020, Pages 1-7

   Endothelial glycocalyx and severity and vulnerability of coronary plaque in patients with *coronary artery disease.*
   Teruyoshi Nemoto

   Conclusions: Lower syndecan-1 level was associated with higher prevalence of vulnerable plaque in patients with CAD. This finding suggests the association between impaired endothelial glycocalyx and the development of vulnerable plaque.

8. Atherosclerosis. 1997 Jul 11;132(1):37-42. doi: 10.1016/ s0021-9150(97)00078-6.

   The effect of the aged garlic extract, 'Kyolic', on the development of experimental atherosclerosis.
   J L Efendy

   In conclusion, 'Kyolic' treatment reduces fatty streak development, vessel wall cholesterol accumulation and the development of fibro fatty plaques in neointimas (inner artery lining) of cholesterol-fed rabbits, thus providing protection against the onset of atherosclerosis.

9. Integr Blood Press Control. 2016; 9: 9–21.

   The effect of aged garlic extract on blood pressure and other ardiovascular risk factors in uncontrolled hypertensives: the AGE at Heart trial.
   Karin Ried, Nikolaj Travica, and Avni Sali
   Our trial suggests that aged garlic extract is effective in reducing peripheral and central blood pressure in a large proportion of patients with uncontrolled hypertension, and has the potential to improve arterial stiffness, inflammation, and other cardiovascular markers in patients with elevated levels. Aged garlic extract was highly tolerable with a high safety profile as a stand-alone or adjunctive antihypertensive treatment.

10. Evid Based Complement Alternat Med. 2013;2013:378657.
    Herbal therapies for type 2 diabetes mellitus: chemistry, biology,

and potential application of selected plants and compounds.
Cicero L T Chang 1

11. PLoS Med. 2008 Feb; 5(2): e45.*b Initial Severity and Antidepressant Benefits: A Meta-Analysis of Data Submitted to the Food and Drug Administration.*
Irving Kirsch

12. Khan A, Redding N, Brown WA (August 2008). "The persistence of the placebo response in antidepressant clinical trials." *Journal of Psychiatric Research.* 42 (10): 791–6 Conclusion: The widely held belief that the placebo response in depression is short-lived appears to be based largely on intuition and perhaps wishful thinking.

13. *Journal of Scientific Exploration*, Vol. 9, No. 2, pp. 223-229, 1995
0892-33 10195

    Psychokinetic Action of Young Chicks on the Path of An Illuminated Source

    Abstract - We tested the possible psychokinetic influence of 80 groups of 15 chicks on a randomly moving robot carrying a lighted candle in an otherwise darkened room. In 71% of the cases, the robot spent excessive time in the vicinity of the chicks. In the absence of the chicks, the robot followed random trajectories. The overall results were statistically significant at $p < 0.01$.

BIBLIOGRAPHY AND RECOMMENDED READING

Campbell, Joseph, *Reflections on the Art of Living: A Joseph Campbell Companion*. New York: Harper Collins, 1991.

Dispenza, Joe, *Breaking the Habit of Being Yourself.* UK: Hay House, 2012.

Gottman, John, "The Roles of Conflict Engagement, Escalation, and Avoidance in Marital Interaction: A Longitudinal View of Five Types of Couples", Journal of Consulting and Clinical Psychology 1993, Vol. 61, No. 1.6-15.

Gottman, John, *The Seven Principles for Making Marriage Work*. New York: Crown Publishing Group, 1999.

Grossman, Michael J. and Barbara R., *The Marriage Map: The Road to Transforming Your Marriage from Ordeal to Adventure*. USA: Silver Torch Press, 2018.

Hunter, Dr. Allan G., *Princes, Frogs and Ugly Sisters: The Healing Power of the Grimm Brothers' Tales*. Scotland, UK: Findhorn Press, 2010.

Kegan, Robert, *The Evolving Self: Problem and Process in Human Development*. Cambridge: Harvard University Press, 1982.

McGilchrist, Iain, *The Master and His Emissary. The Divided Brain and the Making of the Western World*. New Haven: Yale University Press, 2009.

McGilchrist, Iain, *Ways of Attending and How Our Divided Brain Constructs the World*. London: Routledge, 2019.

Schwartz, Mel, *The Possibility Principle*. Boulder, CO: Sounds True, 2017.

Small, J., *Psyche's Seeds,* New York: Putnam, 2001.

Valliant, George, *Adaptation to Life,* Boston: Little Brown and Co., 1977.

Next Steps:
CLASSES AND WORKSHOPS

Discover what it really means to become a wave in your relationship. Grow together in love and understanding as your path unfolds.

Having read this book, you have taken an important step towards ageless love. You are now better prepared to commit to unlocking the passion, love, and deeper connection you know is possible. You understand that working on your relationship is an ongoing part of personal development. Over time it will grow your personality and bring you deeper love and connection.

But it takes the ability to see your partner as an unbound, unlimited wave rather than a fixed entity. This is a key part of the change necessary to create ageless love. Romantic happiness requires continuous attention. It takes skills and practice. It's a journey, with multiple stages to travel through.

Drs. Michael and Barbara promise: When you successfully navigate marriage, ordeal transforms into an odyssey and the waters of life, love, and God open. Michael and Barbara are committed to guiding you to an intimate, romantic partnership filled with passion, joy, enthusiasm, mutual appreciation while dissolving old hurts, resentments, emotional distance and the power struggle.

To help you take that next step, we have special programs designed to guide you on your journey to ageless love.

Use the link below to access our programs.

www.fallinginloveforever.com

Other Books by the Doctors

The Vitality Connection: Ten Practical Ways to Optimize Your Health and Reverse the Aging Process
By Michel J. Grossman, M.D. and Jodi Jones
Vitality Press, 2003

The Magic of Stem Cells: Activating Your Own Healing Power
By Michael J. Grossman, M.D.
Silver Torch Press, 2017

The Marriage Map: The Road to Transforming Your Marriage From Ordeal to Adventure
By Barbara R. Grossman, Ph.D. and Michael J. Grossman, M.D.
Silver Torch Press, 2018

Secrets to Deep and Effortless Meditation: Revealing the Treasures Within
By Michael J. Grossman, M.D.
Salem Press, 2021

About the Authors

ABOUT BARBARA R. GROSSMAN, PH.D.

Dr. Barbara uses her intuition and experience developed over 40 years and 70,000 hours of counseling individuals and couples. She is a master at seeing a couple and knowing what are the next steps needed for their successful journey together.

Dr. Barbara holds advanced degrees from Columbia University and Claremont School of Theology. She has been a Marriage, Family, and Child Therapist since 1986 with an office in Newport Beach, California. She is committed to teaching skills to move couples from emotional distance and power struggle to feeling understood, appreciated and respected. Dr. Barbara's passion is for promoting personal development which is the key to success in life generally, and crucial to the marriage journey.

ABOUT MICHAEL J. GROSSMAN, M.D.

Dr. Michael has been a practitioner and teacher of meditation to thousands of people over 40 years. He has led Attitudinal Healing classes for over 20 years, teaching how to create love, let go of resentments and fear, and how to create an experience of connection to God. He is passionate about using romantic partnership as a vehicle to move couples to higher stages of inner development.

Dr. Michael received his M.D. from New York University, School of Medicine. He works as an anti-aging rejuvenation physician in Newport Beach, California, providing health and longevity through nutrition, bio-identical hormones, sexual dysfunction treatments, stem cells, exosomes, platelet-rich plasma, anti-aging skin treatments, exercise, meditation, and healthy relationships classes.

THE DRS. WORKING TOGETHER

The Drs. say they have had three marriages with each other. The first was ten years of Michael defining the direction of the relationship and Barbara cooperating. The second was a four-year power struggle as Barbara began thinking for herself as she went to graduate school in psychology. The third is a delightful joining of two independent personalities with ever-increasing joy.

When the doctors are not working in their professional capacities in their Newport Beach California office and when they're not writing books or lecturing, they are amateur competitive ballroom dancers. They also perform dance shows which demonstrate the principles of successful romantic partnership.

They have two daughters, two son-in-laws and seven grandchildren.